Diary

# of a Headcase

Diary

of a

Headcase

Faiza Siddiqui

First Printing 2014

ISBN 978-1-291-91806-9

Farhana Haque
The Silverlining Charity
Grapes House
79a High Street
Esher
Surrey
KT10 9QA

www.faizasiddiqui.blogspot.co.uk

Contents

Preface

If you've seen one heart attack, you can say you've seen them all. But if you've seen one head injury all you can say is that you have seen one head injury.

As a result of my head injury, I have come to appreciate that no one can say anything about anybody's brain with any kind of certainty. There are no black-and-white answers, no magic formula to recovery. True, there are broad trends, and our attitudes are formed by studying them. But the nearest that we can come to any sort of understanding comes through the careful listening and sharing of what we have learned with each individual afresh. This is an exercise that begins again for each new head injury as the carers, therapists and survivors all work together. They combine knowledge of how the brain works in general, with the personal story of their experiences.

But we always need to make sure that we listen to what survivors have to say. Only they can tell their story.

This book is my attempt to make sense of what happened to me, so it starts from my first memories after my car crash, to everything that I've experienced since, as well as everything that I've researched to help me make sense of it. I dedicate my book to everyone who has been affected by a head injury: both to the survivors and to those who care for them.

***

When I woke up in hospital I knew I had been there for some time. Exactly how long, I could not tell you - but I knew I had been in a serious car accident and had suffered a massive head injury. I could not make any sense of where I was and what had happened to me. As well as being too brain damaged to think logically, I had lost a year, maybe two. A common symptom of head injuries is lack of insight into their effects. So, I was blissfully unaware of the long, gruelling process that lay ahead of me; I was on a road I hadn't chosen. I have written this book to help me reassemble the scattered pieces.

What I have since come to understand is this: I had moved from London to an Oxfordshire village in August 2008, and 5 months after this I crashed my little car on the way to work. I was left critically ill and in a coma for nearly two months. As a result of the brain damage my memories of the year before the car crash are patchy, if not missing altogether. Forming new memories after the accident was - and still is - difficult.

I remember nothing of the actual crash itself. But what I have been told makes it sound quite dramatic. I am – perhaps absurdly – proud of the theatrical story of which I understand I was the focus. I was driving along a country lane at about 60mph. We will probably never know why but I veered off to the other side of the road. Perhaps it was something as mundane as animal in the middle of the road. My tiny 1.0 litre Toyota Yaris collided with a van coming towards me, and the crash was so serious that it must have looked like a scene from some trashy American drama. I had to be cut out of the car, intubated and airlifted to hospital. In fact, the car was so badly crushed that I had to have plastic surgery on my face. It had been cut by twisted metal from the passenger door – I had been sitting in the driver's seat.

At worst, if I did not make progress, I might have become what doctors call 'brain stem dead', so my body did not have a coughing reflex. As a result, I developed pneumonia, which is what nearly killed me.

Coming out of a coma is nothing like they show in Hollywood. It is a very gradual process of waking up over weeks and months. What Ben, my husband, tells me is that as I slowly learned to talk again, I repeated the single word "obscure" over and over again, almost like a mantra. This is the only direct insight we have into my brain-damaged state of mind: very confused and incredibly unclear. I was not able to form my own memories until several months later, so all we have to go by is Ben's recollection of this single word.

I was diagnosed with a 'diffuse axonal injury', which meant that the damage was spread across my whole brain. I still have trouble with speech and memory, as well as problems with my vision and selective hearing. I also have problems balancing. My speech has improved a lot since the early days, but if you knew me before the accident, you would notice that I sound different. If I am tired the slurring is more noticeable and it sounds as though I am drunk (something that I am not familiar with, being Muslim!).

The injury to my brain had given me reduced insight, so I could not rely on my own sense of who I was. I had no choice but to put all my trust into my family and my therapists, to tell me not only what was happening to me, but also what had already happened (because I was unable to remember). This is why this book is not written solely in my voice: that would not be an accurate reflection of how things were. There were hundreds of different voices telling me what was best for me, how I was affected and what would happen to me. That's why, in this book, I have combined my own diary entries from the time with comments I have written now.

I have learnt that there is nothing to be gained from trying to live up to my image of the 'old Faiza'. I need to live in the here and now. When rebuilding myself I had to face things which I thought I had left behind when I was a teenager. I was just getting past those difficulties but then had to face them again, because they are to do with something fundamental about who I am. Understanding who I am turned out to be a central pillar of my recovery.

***

Throwing myself into my studies was something that had helped me to overcome the depression of my teenage years. Five years after this I found myself studying astrophysics at Cambridge. My mother and father (Ami and Daddy) were perhaps understandably reluctant to send their only daughter to a University away from their home town of London, because they would need to trust me to not run off with a boy who was not of Pakistani descent.

Then in Cambridge, I met a boy called Ben. He was not of Pakistani descent. I kept our relationship a secret from my family, but after a three year degree and a year's teacher training, I realised that this was not a sustainable situation. So, Ben and I decided to get married. I worked as a physics teacher in Camden as we moved around various flats in North-West London. After three years of this, I took a year off to do an MA in education, which I often jokingly referred to as my 'gap year'. Perhaps I had some sort of spooky premonition of the memory loss I would suffer. My whole memory of this time is patchy, and I have only discovered that I had given it this appropriate name after reading my old emails.

I have managed to build a picture of what had happened to my life. I have spent hours trawling through old letters, emails, text messages and my hospital records. I combined them with my own unreliable memories to build up a collage. This picture seems to show that soon after I handed in my dissertation, Ben and I moved. It seems that I had turned to the dark side and started work as a physics teacher in a small private school in Oxford. I built this picture using stories that I have been told by different people, including those who claim that they used to work with me in the few months before the crash. I am now in the process of building a new life for myself: a life for the 'new Faiza'. Although I do not have enough information to make a clear picture of what my life will look like yet, I have learnt about who I am and I've started to have faith that I will be able to build a meaningful life for myself and those around me.

***

This is my story in my own words. It is from my own perspective and this is what I have come to understand about what happened to me.

However, I have changed some names and details to protect people's identities.

***

As Mrs Siddiqui the teacher, I had a method to quickly get the kids out of the busy corridor and into the physics lab with minimal fuss, ready to start work. I would outline a specific routine for entry: go straight to your allocated seat, place your bag under the desk and get your equipment out, ready to start work. You then need to copy the date, title and lesson aims, which I would have ready on the whiteboard.

Because Mrs Siddiqui's rules are hard-wired deep into my brain, I cannot start my book with anything other than a set of aims: I am writing this book to help me discover who the new me is and make sense of my injury. I cannot claim to speak for every single case. I do not even have the ultimate authority to explain what happened for my case. No one does. But this is the best that I can make of what happened.

I have also fallen in love with the brain and this book is a celebration of it: its evolution and how it affects every aspect of who we are.

1   Diary of a Headcase

Monday 27th April 2009

My psychologist reckons that it'll be a therapeutic thing for me to keep a little diary. So this is my psychology homework. Quite why this is therapeutic evades me, but she says it is, so I'll just fill it up.

I guess if nothing else it helps me practice my handwriting. They say that recovering from a head injury is one of the hardest things a person can go through. Well if it is then I think I'm doing quite well actually because this is alright, and I've been through the worst bits.

Although I've probably forgotten the really bad bits. And maybe it's not that bad for me?? I'm not in that much pain. But Ben says that I was in quite a bit of pain back when I was in the JR.

That's the upside to these memory problems: forgetting all the awful things that have happened. They say I've been in hospital for 3 months so far in total, but it feels like I've only been in here for a few days. But at the same time it feels, weirdly, like I've been in here for my whole life.

I guess that might be why the psychologist's told me to keep a diary, so I can keep tabs on time passing by. So, what have I done today? Had this psychology session, where she gave me this notebook. She hadn't prepared anything, yet again.

***

Tuesday 28th April 2009

On my timetable today I thought they had mistyped gym as GPM, but it turns out that it was a "goal planning meeting". So, I went to it, with my "therapy team". To be on my side, Ben was allowed to be there and someone from this charity called Headway.

It felt good to be in a proper grown-up meeting, rather than being treated like a stupid child. But Ben said that the goals they'd set me weren't stretching me enough and I could do better. I guess I never really thought I could question what they said like he does.

Then I had a psychology session and she asked me how I felt the goal planning meeting went. I said how "I felt that the goals weren't stretching me enough." She explained how the goals have been set by professionals, who are experienced in their fields.

I don't really see why I had to be there then, if "they're all experts in the field".

**

The John Radcliffe (JR) is the main hospital in Oxford, and it was to here that I was admitted after the car crash. I have virtually no memories of that time. It was only once I was moved to the Oxford Centre for Enablement (OCE) that I became able to form my own patchy memories. That was when I started keeping this diary.

At the OCE I started learning how to live a life with my new brain, and to "manage my impairments". My affected fine motor control was one of these things: my handwriting was virtually unintelligible. At the time, I was really self-conscious about its quality, which is why I must have it felt necessary to comment on it. For some reason, this was one of the biggest things that I had singled out and deemed necessary to excuse. I guess I saw being in a wheelchair as only a temporary measure.

It was also around this time that I had to start the long process of making sense of what had happened during the time covered by my memory loss. In fact, my latest memories were from 2007-8. The reason I have forgotten events from before the accident was because I was suffering from 'retrograde amnesia', a loss of access to the details of incidents 1-2 years preceding the injury. It was quite unsettling having to take other people's word for things – having a damaged brain never helped with this!

To help me with this task I saw a neuropsychologist, who carried out a cognitive psychological assessment of my brain's abilities. After about a month of doing this testing, I would still have these sessions, but the therapist wouldn't have any pre-prepared exercises. Now she would simply ask me how my week had been. I used to think "She just 'blags it' every lesson", thinking that it was just like when I was a teacher. On rare occasions I might have spent the time preparing a superb lesson, photocopying tailor-made worksheets and starting the lesson with an energetic pupil activity, but at other times I might walk in totally unprepared. She always seemed to do be doing the latter. I guess I felt just like one of my students: patronised by a know-it all, authoritative teacher, who couldn't be bothered to see things from the student's point of view.

To make this feeling of being patronised even worse, I was set goals that my able-brained ally, Ben, told that me "weren't stretching me enough". This was, in fact, not quite the whole truth; it is essential that the goals set in a rehab situation are ones that will be achieved. As a result, they always err on the side of caution and are not made with the primary aim of stretching the patient. Achieving goals helps to give the patient confidence. This was in stark contradiction to the philosophy I always used to set goals for my students: I, like all teachers, always used targets to get them out of their comfort zones.

Feeling that I was being patronised put me in good company: many of my fellow patients at the unit were always complaining about being praised for what used to be inconsequential before they came here. The therapists were probably like this because they knew how people like me tended to lack a sense of achievement, often feeling incapable of performing the most simple of tasks. But the only memories patients had access to were ones formed before the onset of the illness, so they struggled to make sense of the gulf that separated them from their former selves. Would I feel patronised because I could not remember this time, or was it because the therapist struggled to find something to praise me for, so would praise me for something pathetic?

This feeling of being patronised was exacerbated by my affected ability to form new memories: 'ante-retrograde' amnesia. Therapists (and everyone in general actually) would patronise me on the "progress" that I had apparently made. But I wasn't able to remember the time they all referred to, when apparently I couldn't do the simplest of things.

This whole time was made up of recollections of events that were given to me secondhand. So when Ben talked about the pain that I was in at the JR, he was not just talking about physical pain – but my understanding of the concept of pain was limited by the crude conversations that he could have with me at that time. I could not understand the nature of the pain that I had experienced, because it did not fall within my primitive understanding of it. To me, there was no pain other than physical pain. And surely the pain could not have been that bad anyway, because I could not remember it.

I did not understand that the reason I found all this so distressing was that it made no sense to me, which was also why I could not form any memories of it. This was only exacerbated by the fact that I did not think that I was a weak person who could be brought down by her emotions alone. Ben has since talked about the difficulty that I experienced as I came to recognise my disability, and I now feel as though I can appreciate what he was trying to tell me.

Having written this book, I feel like I understand what he was talking about. Anxiety and depression are common to many head injury survivors, and the emotional wellbeing of patients can play an important role in determining brain functioning. There are lots of reasons for this: including having to adjust to a new brain, and dealing with what is often years of lost memories.

As well as understanding what had happened to me, I've had to make sense of the bizarre world of neuro-rehab. I guess that's why I'm writing this book.

***

Wednesday 29th April 2009

Ben was telling me a bit about our lives. It's all so weird. It looks like I've forgotten a fair bit of stuff from before the accident. It looks like I've turned to the dark side and work in a private school now! In Oxford! I guess those kids in Camden must have taken their toll.[1]

I think that does ring a bell somewhere. But I think I've known it all along. Everyone was asking how much of this I remember. Well, nothing.[2]

I properly remember working in Camden though. I also have memories of how Ben hated it in London and we would idly look at jobs outside the M25 on the internet, because we did have some plans to move to the country someday. But I loved it in London. He must have worked some sweet magic on me!

I feel like it was just a few weeks ago that I was a funky young teacher in my early twenties sharing a flat with her bloke in North London. Now I've woken up from this coma to discover that I look like an old lady, have turned to the dark side and live in a posh house in the middle of nowhere.

It's a converted little barn in a tiny village just outside of Oxford. Well, actually it's not so little, Ben showed me some pictures he'd taken to try and jog my memory and it's a proper house![3] It looks really grown up. Not one made for the likes of us. I thought we lived in our little flat in Willesden: it's all well weird.

---

[1] At first, I could not really understand what made the old Faiza "turn to the dark side" and start work at an independent school. I could remember how the students sometimes annoyed me, and how infuriating I would find New Labour's "education, education, education" policy, but I never thought that things were this bad!

When I have since been back to school concerts and the like, I remember that actually it is quite a good school. It has a way of putting a child's wellbeing at the centre of the education he/she receives. That must have been what I loved about it.

[2] Ben had had to tell me repeatedly that we had moved to Oxford. Each time I would forget. Eventually, however, I did manage to become comfortable with this. Since then, I have felt as though I remember our house, but I cannot tell if these are 'lost memories' that I have become able to access again or if these are just fictitious 'screen memories' that I have formed since the accident. Or perhaps, the things I have learnt about my life before the crash, have acted as triggers for the memories that I could not access before.

[3] Ben tells me that these were pictures of our house that he often showed me. Typically, I would forget each time that he had shown them to me. Now, I can only imagine that this would have become increasingly heartbreaking and tedious with each time that it happened.

I read *Forever Today*, Deborah Wearing's account of her husband's devastating amnesia. She writes about some of the traumatic experiences that caring for someone with amnesia can

***

Ben points out to me that the diary entries that I have written here do not present a totally accurate image. When I first came home, I was quite nonplussed apparently by seeing a house that we owned ourselves. I think I must have been so alienated that I was not surprised to find just one more detail of how my life that did not resonate with the sort of person that I thought myself to be.

***

Thursday 30th April 2009

I'm in a new room now. I'd only just got used to my old room being "down the yellow brick road".[4] Now they're sure that I haven't got MRSA,[5] they're making me share. On the way back from dinner today, I forgot where it was. So, I had to stop by the nurses' station and they had to look it up for me.

Ben told me he starts a new job on Monday. I hadn't ever stopped to think "doesn't his job mind him spending all day with me at the hospital?" I guess I just accepted it: "Never look a gift horse in the mouth".

Then in the evening, someone called Samantha visited. She was a teacher at the school I used to work at. She was with someone else I used to work with. They had some cards from some of the kids. We pinned them up on the wall next to all these other cards that it turns out they had brought last time![6] There was one signed by all these kids that I guess I must have taught. It's a big group one, which I'm guessing all the kids were forced to sign.

---

have. My heart sank as it dawned on me that it must have been the same for Ben: that I was a burden on him without knowing it.

[4] The ward was laid out to help patients remember where their bedrooms were. Each of the four differently coloured corridors branched out from the centrally located nurses' station. The number of rooms along each corridor was limited to four and each bedroom had on the door a large printed sign with the patient's name on it. My first room was along the yellow corridor, and to help me remember where it was I would tell myself to "follow the yellow brick road."

[5] Initially all patients are given single rooms because the rehabilitation centre needs to ensure that the patient is able to share a room. This is, to a certain extent, to help control infection. It is also because some patients may not be able to behave in a socially appropriate way and the centre might feel that room sharing may be detrimental to their own rehabilitation, or might cause distress to potential roommates.

[6] Although these cards had been up on the wall all the time, I never took the time to look at them. Part of how the neurological impairments affected my functioning was that although I always knew they were there, I lacked both the curiosity and initiative to read them.

It's quite weird reading all these cards signed by children when they're literally just names. The only names that stand out are unsurprisingly the naughty ones, who had been forced to sign the big group cards. All the little ones signed in nice neat handwriting must be from the good kids. Typically, I can't remember their names. That's not much incentive for them to behave, is it?

When Samantha was here, I made her tea. It's not like a proper hospital here: there's a little kitchen where you can make tea and stuff like that. It's not like the JR:[7] you're free to live your life and have visitors. There's a little garden and we sat out there for a bit. These people from school brought some biscuits, so we had them with the tea.

There were also loads of chocolates that various visitors had brought in the past. They're in danger of going off because I never really eat them. I just have the food like it's medicine. And chocolate is certainly not medicine. I want to get better and protein is what my body needs.[8]

I guess I can't complain because I do get the halal meals. They're always some generic "curry". I don't really know how much better/worse the white people's food is though.

All the patients are forced to sit together, because I think they think it's good for us. But no one ever says a single word. It's kind of like the unwritten rule: have your dinner in silence and be on your best behaviour.[9]

---

[7] The OCE was a rehabilitation centre and not a hospital like the John Radcliffe. Although I could recall the words "rehabilitation centre" to describe this place, I could not appreciate that this was what this made it different from the JR hospital.

[8] During rehab eating started to became something of a chore. Because damage to the pituitary gland had caused a lack of hunger, I had to prioritise what I ate. So I never wasted my precious appetite on carbohydrates, which would fill me up without performing any reparative work. And I certainly would not eat the chocolates that visitors would bring as gifts. But I would always eat the meat, thinking that I needed protein to help rebuild my muscles that did not seem to be working. Protein, however, was not what I needed. Even though I had taught GCSE biology and knew that the brain's damaged axons were not really made of protein, I would force feed myself an entire plate of curry (leaving the carbohydrate) because I was convinced that it was good for me. The nurses would supplement this with Ensure because it was written down as one of my after meal time medicines. Ben teases me about how I became quite overweight.

What I really needed was time, rest and therapy.

[9] Mealtimes are central to patients' rehabilitation. Patients at the OCE often make excellent friends and many find the experience of making friends with people going through a similar experience both rewarding and therapeutic. I suspect that at that stage I was not able to make new friends because of how my social skills had been affected. Other patients probably avoided sitting on my table because I lacked both charm and sensitivity. At the very least, I can say that I was probably no fun for a stranger to be with. Of course, silence abounded because some patients had affected capabilities with language, but I suspect for

So, later I moaned at Samantha about how awful the dinner times are. They make us all sit together, but no one says anything. Some people can't talk, I'll let them off the hook. But those who can, just sit there. I understand some people are naturally quiet or shy, but we all have to make an effort.[10]

Today at dinner I was trying to convince one of the patients, who's always complaining about the food, that he should convert to Islam and get the halal meals, but he declined. I reckon he just prefers to whinge.

***

Friday 1st May 2009

I had an OT cooking session. We did a bit of baking. I couldn't do anything fun because they'd got some cake mix stuff from Sainsbury's that you just add water to. Boring.

Then I had physio. I thought they'd teach me to wheel the wheelchair properly, but no such luck. It looks like they're never going to let me progress onto being able to control this wheelchair.[11] I guess they'd be out of a job if I showed the world that patients can do things themselves.

Fred's going to visit me today. I'll text[12] him to say I'll be in the conservatory. I'll take my iPod & pillow[13] and wait for him there. It'll be nice to show him how I'm making the most of being in this place.

---

many the successful co-ordination of food into the mouth required too much concentration. Holding a conversation was simply too demanding to be an enjoyable experience.

[10] An impaired ability to talk can result from more than just affected physical control over the mouth and tongue. I was unable to appreciate at the time that neurological impairments might impede someone's ability to partake in conversation for reasons other than an 'inability to talk'. A person might be able to produce vocal sounds, but still have difficulty communicating because of other neurological problems. A very readable example can be found in *The Man Who Lost His Language* by Sheila Hale. Here she discusses her experience of her husband's dysphasia. The book is also a lucid general overview of all neuro-linguistic disorders.

[11] I was given a wheelchair to allow mobility as my body learnt to walk again. Even though I had been to my goal planning meeting (where one of my goals was to be able to walk short distances unsupervised a month before discharge) and my physiotherapy sessions were devoted to practicing walking, I could not imagine that I would ever walk again. Because of the way I imagined achievements would progress, I saw the ability to control the wheelchair as a prerequisite for walking later on.

[12] It was only in the last week (before writing this) that I had learnt to send texts. The problem was not really the fine motor control, but managing to think through the operation, despite having a predictive text function!

*****

I think that I had the understanding that at the OCE I would be 'rehabilitated'. I knew that this would involve learning to cope with my disability. I had seen disabled people in the media who functioned independently and being able to control their own wheelchairs appeared to be a fundamental feature of the independent lives they led.

Unaware of my cognitive impairments, I believed that my physical problems were the extent of it. I was unable to appreciate why the OCE would not concentrate all of its available resources on me, helping me be more like one of those functional disabled people on TV. All I thought I needed to do was to learn to use my wheelchair properly, or even better, learn to walk again. I now appreciate that rehabilitation for a head injury survivor is much more complex than just becoming more mobile.

*****

Monday 4th May 2009

I'm just in my room waiting for Ben. Tonight is the first of his "conjugal visits".[14] I hope they make up for something. It's been so crap for him. I was unconscious during the really tough times, and he had to deal with it all alone because I can imagine I was no comfort! But as they say, "the sex is crap, but you can get a good parking space at Asda". So there are both ups and downs to going out with a disabled.

We'll see what this flat is like. It does mean that we can cook our own food, so I don't have to have hospital food. I don't really mind it, but everyone knows how awful hospital food is. I don't want rubbish food: I enjoy a good meal.[15]

*****

---

[13] Whenever I sat somewhere to relax, I would take a pillow with me. At that time, I would get neck pains from straining the tendons that held the weight of my left arm. I was told to rest it on a pillow, so that it would support my arm, rather than pull on the connecting tendons.

[14] The OCE sometimes gives its patients a one-bedroom flat to stay the night with their family, so they can get a bit of privacy and live away from the ward for a while. In addition to the bedroom, there was a small kitchen and a living area, where we'd pretend we were a normal couple.

[15] The hospital food was not the only reason why I couldn't "enjoy a good meal": my sense of smell had been affected, and this took away from my sense of taste.

Although anosmia (a total loss of sense of smell) is rare, hyposmia (a reduced sense of smell) is fairly common amongst head injury survivors. Like many others, I had sustained damage to my olfactory tract, so I had reduced enjoyment of food. However, fine cuisine was something I used to enjoy, and had become part of "old Faiza's" identity. I had to build a new identity for myself that did not require as many functioning neurones.

Tuesday 5th May 2009

I had physio today. I really like Katy [my physiotherapist], even though she goes overboard on the praise. "Well done for reaching for that with your left hand." It's all so patronising: getting praised for using my left hand! I never got praised for this kind of stuff before. I said this to her, and she said that it is an achievement for me, "considering how far you've come."[16]

Is that how achievements work then? So, we don't just say well done based on how big the achievement is, but on whether it's an achievement for that <u>particular</u> person. I mean, what kind of achievement is that? But if they say it is an achievement, then I guess I'll just have to accept it.

Then I had pottery. Carried on with some plant pot that they say I've been making for the last couple of weeks.

Then in the evening Ben's parents [Carol and David] came. Carol brought some Immac wax strips because she said how last time I was complaining about the wash & dress sessions, and how people can't deal with the fact that I'm a mammal.[17]

So she helped me wax my legs. Now they [my legs] are a bit more socially acceptable.

***

Wednesday 6th May 2009

I had a wash & dress session this morning. They gave me an "adapted method", so that I could do my bra up with my crap hands.[18] They showed me a method that little kids use

---

[16] Like many head injury survivors I would often feel patronised by people, and also lacked a sense of achievement, because of my memory problems. Would I feel patronised because I could not remember a time when I could not do this, or was it because the therapist struggled to find something to praise me for, so would have to patronise me?

[17] I have always enjoyed affirming my womanhood, in spite of hair growth, by reminding people of the fact that body hair is one of the characteristic features of mammals. I did not really mind being hairy, and used to hope that admission to hospital and having affected motor control would act as sufficient excuse for me to neglect the finer aspects of my self-beautification regime. For me, the collective nature of the effort needed just to wax my legs was somehow symbolic of the collaborative, decentred nature of my recovery. Instead of simply waxing my legs on my own like a normal person, my body was transformed through the combination of my own efforts with those of others. And I was not even that bothered in the first place about how "bad" they looked when hairy; I just thought that I should do it because of other people's reactions to my mammalian legs.

[18] Tighter shoulder and arm muscles, reduced sensation in my fingers and reduced fine motor control combined to make it impossible for me to do up my bra using the 'normal' method. Now I have to fasten the hooks at the front and THEN swivel it round. Before, I

to do up their first bra. I don't want to learn some stupid adaptation, I want to spend time doing exercises to get my arm working properly again.

I'll just go along with it. They're not making it worse I suppose.

I think that's why they say it takes a long time – it's because they waste time doing this sort of thing. But there's only one way to get better: they should be spending the time on physio to make my arm good again, not just making some pointless adaptations. But then they'd be out of a job and we couldn't have that could we?[19]

Last night Fred came to visit. I pointed out the nurse who I thought was just right for him. He said he thinks that he's not bad. I think I'll ask some other nurse if this nurse is gay, rather than go up and just put my foot in it. I'll say "I know some guy and I reckon you two would make a really cute couple." And then he'll turn around and say, "What, a queer? Uurgh! That's gross." They do say I'm socially unaware, so I'll show them this time and I'll check with some other nurse if he's actually gay (and not just camp), before I go and incite their little judgements.

I was telling Fred about my "disinhibited" behaviour, and he found it all quite funny. I just think it's comical how they use all these special head injury words to just describe my normal behaviour. Like, my "wash and dress" sessions are hilarious. True, I might say cunt a fair bit, but that's just what it's called.

Anyway, it was fun seeing him. We had hot chocolate that Ben brought for me for when I'm entertaining visitors.

---

would need no such adaptation: my unimpaired arms could reach between my shoulder blades whilst remaining dexterous enough to fasten two pairs of small metal hooks.

[19] All patients recovering from a head injury need to learn adapted methods to perform functional tasks in order to stimulate the brain to optimise its functioning in the long term. I now appreciate that my injury was not an illness that would 'just' get better. The Occupational Therapy that I received had been tailored to give the maximum benefit to a person who had survived a brain injury: it struck a balance between working towards recovery, and living with impairments that were never realistically going to go away completely. At the time I did not appreciate that not all of my impairments would get better.

Friday 8th May 2009

It's Friday today. Ben says he has his half-day on Fridays, so he'll be here in a bit. Then I've got physio and I'll sneak him in. Apparently they used to like him coming to my physio sessions when I was in the JR, but the physio here's not so keen[20].

In the morning I had woodwork. I'm making this bookend for Ben. I like being in the workshop. Feels just like the one they had at school. We actually get to do something productive rather than the stuff they make us do at "upper limb group", where they get us to make up a glass of squash using my cripple hand and then drink it (always with the "impaired limb").

Saturday 9th May 2009

Chris came to visit today. And then Naveed, Erum [my brother and his wife] and their little baby, Humza. Naveed's become a dad! Apparently the baby was born about 6 months before the car crash. And they say I even went to see them in Birmingham [where Erum's parents' house is] after she'd given birth. And they say they've all visited me here before. I guess they must have done.

Humza's on the verge of walking. I was saying, "I wonder who'll learn to walk first: me or Humza?" Naveed laughed and said I would, but I reckon it'll be quite close. I can't even control my wheelchair at the moment. But I guess he was just being nice.

They let me go out to this little park across the road. I guess they could let me because I was with some "normals". There's a little garden here and I think there were quite a lot of green spaces around the hospital when I was in the JR, but it was so fun to be out in the real world: not some safe, gated-up little space, which they call a garden to delude you into believing that it's the real world.

Sunday 10th May 2009

Ben's family visited today. They asked the hospital if they could take me out for a meal, so we went to some pub over the road. We drove because they said it'd be too much for me to walk. I didn't want to pollute the atmosphere, but they made me [go by car].

It also turns out that we have two little kittens! Ben says we got them a couple of weeks before the crash. It sounds like we're proper grown-ups. His parents said that they're taking them home with them because Ben's going to stay with them. Apparently it's too

---

[20] When I was in the JR, because of my condition, I found it difficult to focus without Ben's calming presence. However, by the time I had been admitted to the OCE my cognition had developed to the point that Ben's presence had now become an active distraction.

far to commute from our house to his work in London. They say that the cats shouldn't be left alone in the house all that time.

Ben told me that we named them Blackberry and Cobweb. Aw, that's cute. They brought them here to the OCE. I did tell Ben's family they're all quite nice and laid back here and we could sneak two little kittens into my room, but they just had to play it safe: they wouldn't believe me and they kept them outside in the garden.

Then afterwards, they sneaked me home! The nurses assumed that I was still at the pub with the grown-ups.

Monday 11th May 2009

Just had my halal dinner and worryingly I found it quite hot!! My chilli tolerance has virtually gone. It wasn't that long ago when we went to India and I would laugh at how weak and white Ben's tongue was, always bragging that all sensitivity in my tongue had been burned out by years of Ami's saalan [Mum's Pakistani curries]. I guess this would only be classed as a minor side effect of being in a coma. Not being able to walk would probably rank a little higher!

I also had a little chat with Jane [one of my OTs] and she said that they'll let me home to stay for one night a week before I get released (or "discharged", as she prefers to call it). She doesn't see the funny side of the whole release/discharge thing.

She said that she'd talk to Ben about having a little visit to check if it's safe and if they need to put any ramps in etc. I almost said "You don't need to because I've already been", but I didn't give the game away (they might reconsider my privileges if they find out). So she said I might be able to go home (legitimately!) for my birthday party.

Wednesday 13th May 2009

Ben's on a half day today and he's going to pick me up in a bit and take me home for the night. I'll finally get to be in a private little space of our own. People say I used to have my own private room, but not anymore. I guess when they deem you well enough to be inflicted on other people, then you lose all your privileges.

Even though the girl I share my room with isn't bad, she is still someone else. Sometimes me and Ben should have some privacy. I don't really mind, but he's so shy about these things. He's always saying "What if someone comes in?" Well, we're allowed to smooch - we are married. I tell him that we can pull the curtain round,[21] but he doesn't listen.

Thursday 14th May 2009

Some people came to see me when I was in a session. This time they were from Summertown [college][22], so they had a reason for not liaising with my PA[23] to visit me while I was in physio.

It made me think that I need to find a way of getting my timetable "out there". I hate to say it, but I've been thinking that Facebook might be the best way. Najma said she'd get me an account, and today when I logged onto my hotmail there were millions of emails from Facebook! Bless her, when Ami [Mum] saw them she asked "Facebook kawn hai?" [Who's Facebook].

After that, I went home in the car with Hannah and Katy [my OT and my physiotherapist]. They said that they'd organised with Ben that they'd take me home.

They looked round and said it was all OK. Yeah, I know - I've been there! I was so excited thinking that we might wangle a Stannah stair lift, but they said that they were just looking to see if they needed to put in hand rails in the bathroom. They said all the steps were fine and if I don't feel up to it, I can hold Ben's hand.

It's all so exciting: they FINALLY trust me enough to stay at home. Not "home alone", though. Only good children are allowed that.

Friday 15th May 2009

I just had physio. We practiced walking without the zimmer frame Katy says I've got to focus on the quality of my steps and not try and rush it. I can't be bothered to consider

---

[21] In the bedroom there was a curtain that one could pull around the bed for privacy while getting undressed. I was not sympathetic when Ben objected, saying he did not feel as though we had privacy. I was not fussed - a lack of desire for privacy comes under the banner of disinhibited behaviour, which is common for head injury survivors.

[22] Summertown College was the school I worked at in Oxford.

[23] At this time I would often jokingly call Ben my PA because he would liaise with friends and family in order to manage visiting times. I could not organise this myself because it would require me to manage dates and times, as well as to give directions and to explain hospital rules and routines, which I was fairly oblivious of. This was a new role for Ben, because until now I had always been the more organised one.

EACH step. I just want to walk. Normal people don't have to "consider the quality of their steps", so why should I? I don't just want to <u>look</u> normal, I want to <u>be</u> normal. [24]

It's funny they call the physio room a gym. I guess it sort of is. But it's not full of muscle men like normal gyms are. It is nice they call it a gym, though, to make it all feel like a simulation of the real world. Like the OT "kitchen" is an actual kitchen with a cooker and oven in it, and yet it's somehow not. There's something about this place, like it's a "mock real world". But no one ever admits to us that it's all essentially mock.

I'm so looking forward to being allowed into the real world tomorrow. I know this is quite nice as hospitals go, but it's still a hospital. It's not my own place. There's something psychological about it. It's all property of the NHS. It's not property of Faiza-Ben.

---

[24] The rollator is a walking frame on wheels. I often called it a zimmer frame because this seemed to articulate my feeling of having aged prematurely. (It was essentially a zimmer frame on four wheels.) As time passed by, I no longer 'needed' it to walk, but Katy would still advise me to use it. She said I should focus on the quality of my steps not just so I would 'look normal', but to ensure that I would not damage my muscles by learning to walk in a way that would result in injuries. I never saw why I should use it, despite being told all this quite explicitly. As a result of my head injury I could not take anything in. Despite having understood the words Katy said, I failed to grasp their significance. I needed to be told again and again because this new information failed to mesh with my former conceptions (or what educational psychologist Jean Piaget might call my "previously existing schemata").

2   Rehab

The OCE is a specialist rehabilitation centre for people with long-term neurological conditions. Patients are there for all sorts of reasons, including head injuries and strokes as well as a variety of less common conditions. The centre works to enable those with long-term neurological illnesses to live a fulfilling life with their conditions.

The entrance takes you through a large, automatic and cripple[25]-friendly sliding door into an airy reception area. On the wall there is painted a mural of an outdoor scene with flowers and butterflies, like a typical English garden in summertime.

Through a set of double doors off to the side is the ward, and there is a large dining hall where the patients have their meals. I can't remember the first time I went there, but I've been told about how on my first night, I sat eating and making polite conversion with the other crips. I think I remember trying not to get too distracted as I saw Ben walk past with his parents. Now he tells me about this from his perspective: he says how he felt a mixture of pride and anxiety, watching me as I "took your [my] first faltering steps into what was going to be the rest of your [my] life."

Then, adjacent to the dining hall is a social area, where we could watch TV or read any of the newspapers or books that were dotted around. Patients are encouraged to be independent, so there is a kitchen where we could use the microwave or make a cup of tea. Sometimes, some patients are given keys to the flat, either to spend time with family or to help them live independently as they get closer to their discharge date. Round the back there is a conservatory which opens out onto the garden. It is maintained by the patients' OT gardening club.

When I first got to the OCE I was given a room which looked out onto this garden. Patients tend to be given single rooms when they first arrive, before they are well enough to share. Each shared room has yellow walls, a pine wardrobe, a

---

[25] I feel the need to justify my use of the word "cripple"... It is used by some disabled people to re-appropriate their disability as part of a positive identity. I had, and to a certain extent still have, to live a life in a rubbish body. Unashamedly celebrating its shortcomings by calling myself a crip has been central to this. As I "recover", I'm less and less sure about whether it's still acceptable for me to use that word. When I didn't need a wheelchair, I could justify using it because I had to use a stick. But after that I was only a wobbler – where's the cut-off point?

bedside table and a shared chest of drawers. They are all en-suite with a toilet and shower, which both have handrails. Both my bedrooms were as much like home as a hospital room could be.

All the patients' bedrooms are downstairs, near the social area. Then there is a lift to go upstairs to where the therapy rooms are. Or, you could take the stairs. The stairs are often used for physiotherapy, so patients can practise walking up and down stairs. The therapy rooms include a gym, an art room, a kitchen and a workshop. This is where I had my occupational therapy. You can also find doctors' and therapists' offices, consultation rooms and meeting rooms. These consultation rooms were where I would have my psychology or speech and language sessions.

I always felt that the NHS was spending an excessive amount on my rehabilitation because they inexplicably believed that I was ill and this would make me better. I thought, "If they want to spend money on buying me paint and paying for pottery lessons, then I'm not going to be stupid enough to argue with them." I was unable to grasp that a patient's calm and happy state of mind has a tremendous influence on the success of brain rehabilitation, which is why they were buying me all this paint and clay. Looking back, it stands to reason that activities which engage patients are more successful than routine and laborious ones. "But", I used to think, "there's hardly anything wrong with me, anyway."

I have fond memories of my time there and I think it was a happy one. By the time I was able to form new memories of my stay at the OCE, my brain was able enough to engage with life. Living, for now at least, was a pleasant experience. Also, my brain was still too damaged to make sense of what was wrong with me. I had no real idea that I would not be able to return to work immediately. My only fear was that the school would give me the sack, motivated by disability prejudice alone.

Our house is now filled up with all sorts of things I made when I was ill. There are pictures, paintings, models and sculptures. The place is adorned with my "cripple creations".

***

This is the first email that "the new Faiza" sent, presumably from the OCE patient room:

To: Benjaminsmith
Date: Mon 24/04/2009 13:24
Subject: RE: Hellooo

hello
 youre zo kind.
ghank u so much dor sticking by me & all ur kindness in the last few week.
lu u
Faiza

The high frequency of typos is because of my affected fine motor control and the head-injured patient's lack of attention to detail. The email also seems to resonate with Ben's claims that during my time in hospital and rehabilitation I was extraordinarily grateful for even the smallest of kindnesses. When he tells me how much effort composing and typing this would have been, this email certainly confirms this. I can see for myself that it was written at a time when my memory was so affected that I mention the kindness I have received "in the last few week", at a date which is nearly 3 months after the crash. This email is one of the few windows that I have into my experience of the world at that time.

Not being able to form accurate memories is a common problem that patients face. Having experience of how this can affect people, my psychologist gave me a diary to keep. I diligently wrote in it nearly every day, earnestly believing that this was one of the things that would help people deem it feasible for me to return to my life in the able-bodied world. Later, over a year after discharge, I read it expectantly in the hope that it would be a window into my soul at that time.

I was horribly disappointed: it was appallingly written. As well as being virtually unintelligible (having been written with my crippled hands), it has barely any mention of my feelings. At best, it was a factual record of my rehabilitation treatment. So I have had to re-write the diary entries that are included here – using the information and insights that I have collated from a variety of different sources. The entries I have written for dates after my discharge use cuttings from emails I sent at the time.

Despite its numerous shortcomings, I was able to glean a few insights from this diary. One of the most frequent words to appear was "apparently": drawing my attention to how I was forced to accept what people said to me, even when I could not make any sense of them. This was not limited to the things that I had already been told, but also the things I had said, what I felt and how I had behaved. This applied to all sorts of things and continued for some time after my discharge.

Gradually I became able to form more accurate memories for myself. (But even these memories are not 'normal' and were certainly not as clear as the memories that the 'old Faiza' would have made.)

In addition to the diary lacking emotional insight, it seems to be plagued by a handful of thoughts, which recurred on a cycle. The main one was that I felt horribly patronised. This was normally because I had achieved something that I had not been able to do when whoever I was talking to saw me last. I, however, could not perceive this time gap, and did not think that whatever physical feat I had performed was anything especially praiseworthy: I felt that I had been given my own special criteria, which had been adjusted for my "disability".

Another thing that my diary showed me was that my intrapersonal intelligence had been affected. I had little insight into myself and found it difficult to make sense of my disability. A lack of insight is common for many head injury survivors. It is called anosognosia, and refers to the survivor's lack of awareness of the very existence of their own disability.

Those who confuse it with the defence mechanism of denial need to peruse the wealth of literature exploring anasognosia[26]. There they would discover that, in fact, it can be associated with neurological damage to the parietal lobe and ranges from the very dramatic to the more subtle. At the dramatic end of the spectrum, the survivor might be unaware that she is blind or paralysed; at the more subtle end, she might be unaware of some cognitive impairments. Although my new head presented me as a relatively mild case, it was no exception.

By the time I had returned home I had a good appreciation of my physical impairments. (Although it was by no means perfect: there are plenty of broken plates and glasses which can vouch for this.) Awareness of my cognitive impairments, however, could at best be described as patchy.

I had always taken it for granted that it was part of my personality that I was 'emotionally intelligent'. The 'old Faiza' was well endowed with both inter- and intra-personal intelligence: she could read both her own emotions and other people's. The new me was not quite so blessed.

During my life, especially in my time reading physics at Cambridge, I had certainly come across people who were very clever but who were illiterate when it came to

---

[26] When describing anosognosia in *Phantoms in the Brain*, the popular neuroscientist, Vilayanur Ramachandran, writes that "something's wrong, but you'll never know why."

social signals. To these physicists these signals must have seemed so hair-splittingly subtle as to be undetectable, but to me, they always seemed obvious. I have now come to appreciate that being 'emotionally intelligent' is nothing to pride yourself on; it is simply the result of your neurological wiring. It is no more a product of your will than the colour of your eyes or the dryness of your skin.

My time in rehab was a confusing one: I never understood why people around me were behaving so oddly. I just put down incidents with other patients to their own personal problems. "Perhaps he's facing his own mortality." I was unable to see things from their perspective (I was unable to 'decentre'). It never occurred to me that they might be facing emotional difficulties, or that they were unable to compute my actions because they had suffered a brain injury themselves. When staff seemed annoyed at me I put it down to the fact that nursing is a stressful job, or that the therapists just treated me differently because they could not see past the inappropriate labels they had tagged me with. I am, I thought, quite an easy person to get on with.

I only had these thoughts occasionally because I was nearly always busy: occupied in therapy sessions, doing my exercises, or 'entertaining' visitors. But I did have them: usually just before I fell dead to the world at night. Here is another email that I sent, that seems to corroborate my memories of this time:

To: Najma Warsi
Date: Thu, 9 Jul 2009 19:29:33 +0000
Subject: RE: Welcome back

Forgive the stupid font and the typos. They're because of my double vision and poor finger controll (respectively). I hear that you might be up for a visit at some point. So let me say when I can fit you into my busy schedule...

I go home at the weekend and its usually quite bu[s]y with people (mainly family coming to visit) and the next 2 weekend (thats a 3 day weekend) are booked with 1. Going to see Leonard Cohen 2. My nephew's birthday party up in Birmingham. Tuesdays and Wednesday nights I get to go home with Ben and give him a good seeing to whether hes in the mood or not.

During the days I'm quite busy with therapy sessions. For more details go to my facebook page. I bebrudgingly joined facebook[27] because it was the best way to

---

[27] In fact, it was Najma who set up a Facebook account for me, after I asked her a few weeks previously. The reason that I refer to my joining Facebook as "begrudging" was because I often talked about my dislike of it. I saw it as nothing more than a popularity

spread my timtable to the masses. I plan in [sic] unjoining as soon as I get released (or "discharged" as they prefer to call it). Any plans you do make run them past my PA (or Ben as he prefers to be called). I think thigs [sic] have come to an all time low if I have to rely on HIM to organise ME.

Hear from you soon.

Love Faiza

***

Even though there was lots going on, I can tell you little about it because my memory of the time in rehab is quite patchy. Because my awareness of the passage of time was poor, Ben got me into the habit of crossing days off the calendar when they passed. This helped me gain a sense of time moving forward. I used to joke how it was like being a prisoner, counting how many days of my sentence had passed. But I don't really remember much for at least my first month (or two) there.

When I ask Ben or read old emails it can feel a little familiar. I have done this so often that I can't tell if these are really 'my memories' or what Freud calls 'screen memories'. I think that I do remember my parents visiting, though.

The OCE understood the impact of not only the patient's engagement with their disability, but also the importance of family's involvement with the rehabilitation process. Another patient, Brian, loved Indian food. He constantly craved a good curry and wanted to cook some Indian food in his OT cooking sessions. So Jane, after seeing how my parents visited virtually every day, asked Ami if she would be happy to teach him one of her recipes and team teach a cooking session for him.

Unsurprisingly, Ami leapt at the opportunity. We had a session where both Brain and I worked with Ami to cook some aloo-gobi.

***

---

contest (who could get the most "friends"). When I was at university, I was always very vocal about my dislike of 'sites like this. Nowadays, I am a big advocate of social networking and feel that it can help people to have a voice: people who might be alienated from mainstream media. Because I have seen their value to disabled people to help them feel less isolated, I have backtracked on my earlier opinions.

Every week the OCE issued me with a timetable of my activities. Using the IT skills I had learnt after years of working as a physics teacher (making my own worksheets), I would produce an image of my timetable and upload it to my Facebook wall. (Because Facebook was new to me, Ben wrote me a set of instructions about how to navigate the site, which I kept in a filofax which the OTs had given to me.)

I also have memories of Ben visiting me in the OCE and not being able to have much privacy. After I had been there for a month, I no longer had the privilege of an individual room. He had prohibited me from "expressing too much affection" for him when we were not alone. I remember that sometimes we would go out to sit in the car, so that we could be away from people.

Out in the car Ben felt that he could talk with me and open up. He tells me that on one of these occasions, he gave me some basic mental arithmetic to do. I used to think these sums were mental exercises that would make me better. I worked on them with the simplistic and incorrect principle that "the brain is a muscle; using it will make it stronger". I was unable to appreciate that he set these sums so that he would be able to assess the effects of the head injury for himself.

Recently, he recounted how I was unable to do some of them, bringing tears to his eyes. He told me how I comforted him "so kindly", saying that he was calmed, but that this was all tainted by the fact I had no inkling of why this was all so significant in the first place. I think I must have thought things had just got on top of him. I often joked, to myself, that it had, after all, been a difficult time for Ben: apparently, his wife had been very seriously injured in a car crash...

***

I don't really remember this particular wash and dress OT session, but I do remember that the OTs did these sessions with me. Unlike most of the patients, it never really bothered me having to be naked in front of relative strangers. "It's part of their job." OTs taught me how someone with crap hands/impaired upper limb functioning could do up her bra. They would also advise me to use my impaired limb to help lather the shampoo or shower gel. I mention one of these sessions in an email:

To: Nicola Thomson
Date: Sat 02/05/2009 20:59
Subject: RE: Hello!

Hi Nicki,

It was lovely to hear from you.

I thought you might appreciate this. Ben told me that when I was coming out of my coma that the physio kept on saying "Can you do this with your hand?", and I'd say, "I can't", and she said, "Oh no, yes you can." After a while I said, "I'm not Jane

Wilkins[28]", meaning I'm not a hypochondriac. Obviously I associate Jane quite deeply with being a hypochondriac. Maybe they uncovered some sort of Freudian connection.

I quite like it when people tell me stories about my antics when I was in a coma. They tend to stay off the topic, anticipating that it will upset me, but it has quite the opposite effect!

I'm quite looking forward to the activities but I'm not sure how many I'll have. At the moment I've only had woodwork. First job: laying laminate floors! Only kidding.[29]

I remember when you and Alex came to visit me. Gemma and Si went to Posh Fish today too. Si couldn't finish his fish and chips either. Tell Alex that he must have a small dick (Si, not Alex).

Also, after having used the word 'cunt' inappropriately Ben said I should use the phrase "the c-word" to cover it up. When I was in the shower the other day, she had to shower gel my "nether-regions", and when she finished she complemented the smell of the shower gel, and I just said, "Next time my husband goes down on me, I'll tell him the scent is a treat from you." She didn't say much in response.

See you soon,

Faiza

("Madame disinhibited" - scribed & obscenity-checked by Ben)

***

When I behaved like this the OTs would issue me with a "yellow card". This is the system that they used with patients who needed to relearn what was socially acceptable. So whenever I said something like this, the therapist would alert me in a light-hearted way that it was socially unacceptable, by saying "YELLOW CARD".

---

[28] Jane Wilkins is a university friend of ours, who was known for being something of a drama queen.

[29] In my woodwork sessions I made a book end for Ben. The reason that I over compensated for my ironic tone with frequent use of exclamation marks and explicitly stating that "I'm only kidding" was because I was becoming aware that there was some sort of problem with people picking up on when I was being sarcastic: patients never laughed at my gags and the nurses were even worse. I began to put this down to some kind of notion that my personal sense of irony was excessively attuned.

"But I've always been like this," I would say. I explained how I'd never been one to 'play it safe' and enjoyed playing with the boundaries of what society deems as acceptable behaviour. I had always found it a source of amusement.

"They just don't have a clue," I thought.

The OTs had explained to me that I was displaying disinhibited behaviour. Disinhibition, they explained, is a common behaviour associated with a head injury. The most famous case is probably Phineas Gage: he was the first recorded survivor of a severe brain injury. Neurological textbooks refer to him as the "American Crowbar Case".

On September 13, 1848, when he was 25 years old, the construction worker was working on the railroad. He was blasting a path to clear it, when a colleague distracted him and he accidentally dropped the metre long iron rod he was using on some gunpowder. It shot up to penetrate his head and went straight up through his skull. It landed some 25 metres away, "smeared with blood and brain." He seemed unharmed and was speaking within a few minutes. But he was never the same again. Most of his left frontal lobe[30] was destroyed, he suffered from epileptic seizures and his friends described him as "no longer Gage"[31].

His personality was transformed. The contractors felt that he went from being "the most efficient and capable foreman" on the railroad, to a man who could no longer get along with anyone. Biographies, written by able-brained third parties, often describe him as wishy-washy and vague one moment, then irritable and emotionally unstable the next. He drank, was short-tempered and swore much more frequently. The doctor analysed the new Phineas as someone whose "equilibrium between his intellectual faculties and animal propensities" was destroyed. In fact, this was so profound that the contactors gave him the sack.

But, I still had a point: they didn't have a clue. All people could see were deviations from 'the norm'.

---

[30] The frontal lobes were the last part of the brain to evolve and are, broadly speaking, what makes humans human. They work as the control centre of the brain, enabling an individual's 'executive functioning'. Executive functioning is an umbrella term for cognitive processes such as planning, predicting and the monitoring of actions.

[31] A good discussion of Phineous Gage can be found in *Descartes' Error: Emotion, Reason and The Human Brain* by Antonio Damasio, 1994.

Even when I was in the JR, staff were already concerned about my disinhibited behaviour. Ben tells me how sometime in March 2009, he arrived to be taken aside by a concerned nurse and was told how the night before, I had continually asked to be changed into my pyjamas. The evening before he left, Ben had only changed my bottoms, leaving me in my tight superman T-shirt.

Apparently, from what Ben tells me, the nurse said I was uncomfortable and repeatedly asked to be changed into my pyjamas. Knowing I was a head case, he told me that I was already in my pyjamas. I explained to him that these were not my pyjamas, adding, "If these are my pyjamas, then why am I wearing a bra?", lifting up my top to show it to him.

I did not have one on.

Much to my mother's disappointment, I have never been particularly ashamed of my body. In spite of all I had been taught about the importance of shame (sorry, 'modesty'), I was quite happy lifting up my top to show my bra to a male nurse. I had just forgotten that Ben had slipped it off before going home.

My shoulders always ache, and no doubt it was worse back then, so it must have felt as though I was wearing this instrument of torture that society dictates women must wear at all times. But in the nurse's eyes this was a textbook display of 'disinhibited behaviour': something he could note down, tick a box and get concerned about. I'm not so sure. True, if one of the non-brain-damaged staff had behaved like that, it might have been 'disinhibited'. But for me, it was a logical way of showing him that I had a bra on, that I needed to take off. The only thing head-injured about it all was that I had forgotten that I did not have one on.

In rehab I was surrounded by people all the time (and I was much better, comparatively). The nurses would have listened to me when I said I needed to have my bra off. In fact, I was even shown how I could do this myself. I was in a world where every detail had been thought about. I was always busy. Everyone was kind. I felt loved. But, I was alone: no one shared my view of the world. Even though I was at the centre of everything, I had it all wrong.

3 Diary continued

Saturday 16th May 2009

Writing this at home. Ben's in the kitchen clearing up after family came over for my birthday. I think my birthday lands in the week, so we're milking it for the 2 weekends either side: family this weekend and friends the next. I'm allowed home to spend the night here for it.

I've done really well out of this birthday. This is one of the advantages of nearly dying: everyone's so grateful for your life. I should be in a coma every year!

Ami brought all the food because she said it'd be too much for me to cook. Well, I'm not complaining. May as well milk my illness for all it's worth. Ben's a bit useless in the kitchen anyway[32].

And Naveed got me an iPod!! It's got a really large memory to volume ratio - must have been pricey. Things have come on quite a bit while I was in my coma: you can put videos on this one now, apparently. Classic Ami got me stuff from the practical department: clothes that I can wear when I'm in sessions at the OCE.

***

Sunday 17th May 2009

Back at the OCE now. Had a lazy morning with Ben. It always used to be a problem that I used to wake up before Ben, but today I slept in longer than him![33]

We took the rollator home, but I never used it: it's just dead weight. Ben reckons it's not safe for me to go to the toilet without him holding my hand, but I never waited for him. Sometimes I genuinely forgot, but then after I forgot I realised that I can make it by myself. When he found out he really told me off. "What if you had a turn and fell?" Well I didn't, did I?

---

[32] The most vivid memory I had of Ben's cooking skills is when we were at university and he was proud that he cooked me a meal of chilli con carne with some boil in the bag rice. When I came home and he cooked for me I was quite taken aback that "he had learned to cook while I was in my coma." He had just been slowly learning over the years, but I had never refined my judgment of him. It kills me to say that he is, now, by far the better cook.

[33] I slept much longer than Ben because I was affected by fatigue, which is often cited as one of the major impairments that a head injury survivor has to live with.

***

Monday 18th May 2009

Had physio today. We practiced walking without the frame. I don't really need it that much anymore anyway. I find it more of a hassle. Like that time in my old room[34].

I'm writing my diary because no-one's due to visit and I don't really know how to pass the time when I'm by myself.[35] I think I'll ask Suzy [my psychologist] if there are any exercises I can do to train up my brain. But while I wait for it to heal I guess I'll just have to chat to people and watch trash TV to occupy myself. I just wish it would just heal a bit quicker.

But because no one was going to visit tonight, Ben organised for Najma to call me. But chatting does leave me at the mercy of people's "helpful" words. She quite upset me while we were chatting. I was telling her about how I find the physios and OTs quite patronising because they always praise me for the tiniest of things.

So she "sympathised", saying her experience of neuro-rehab left her feeling that therapists were incredibly patronising to patients. And then she said, "But I can see you're still not the old Faiza." Can you believe that?! [36]

---

[34] The "time in my old room", refers to a memory I had of a time when my rollator got stuck between the wall and the bed, when I was in my first room at the OCE. I was not physically able to climb up onto the bed and reach for the little buzzer to call the nurses. I did, however, manage to get to my mobile on the bedside table, phoned Ben in a panic, and he called the nurses' station for me. This prompted me to get Ben to feed the number for the nurse's station into my phone. However, becoming trapped by my walking frame never happened again.

[35] I found it difficult to pass the time because of the combined effects of various impairments. The result was that I had to adjust to how my brain processed the information my senses provided. For example, before my head injury I would pass a rainy afternoon by watching a film or reading a novel, but now I couldn't do this. The effects of my cruder impairments are easier to understand: double vision made reading difficult, jumbling and scattering words haphazardly across the page. Most people can see how memory problems would have affected my love for reading involved Victorian novels. But even after I had worn an eye patch, I was unable to process and make sense of even short stories or magazine articles. The words just would not make much sense. Even my sense of taste, smell and vision had also been affected. So, I was not able to gain the same enjoyment from chomping on a Mars bar or looking at photographs. Time trickled by slowly, and I had no way of making it run faster.

[36] I have since raised my memory of this conversation with Najma, but she says she does not remember it, which in itself speaks volumes about my 'impaired memory'. (Memory is, by definition, selective: each time a memory is played back in 'the mind's eye', it is reinforced.) I can only surmise that it must have been painfully awkward for people around me to cope with the additional neurological symptom of lack of insight into the disability. I have since learned that all relationships can be affected by a brain injury, not just family and

The more I think about it, the more upset I feel. It's a bit yin-yang: being praised for pathetic little things, like they're huge achievements. Then being told "I'm still not the old Faiza". Who's right?

I thought I am still me, but she says I'm not, so there must be something wrong. Or is she just being fussy, because there's nothing really up apart from my speech? Oh yeah, and memory. And even that's up to a day now.[37]

None of the physios and OTs who bandy about praise so freely knew the old Faiza, so how can I trust what they say? And it is part of their job to be positive anyway. But they are professionals. But maybe these are achievements for people in the general population? I never thought that I was such a snob!!

Maybe there is something wrong with me, but because of this car crash, people don't like to focus on it. They think they should just be pleased to see me alive. I feel so ungrateful: other people are just happy that I'm alive, but I want to have more than just to be. Is that wrong?

Tuesday 19th May 2009

It's my birthday today. Ben'll be here in a bit, so I'm doing some psychology homework before he gets here! Everyone keeps being polite and felt obliged to chit-chat and ask me how old I am. But I just tell them I don't know. Then I started thinking, I hope they don't think that I'm ashamed of my age, so I've just started to say "I was born in 1982, work it out.[38]*"*

We've booked to have the OCE flat as a bit of a treat. My family and some of Ben's family are all due soon to help me do my birthday. I still had to have physio and OT though: there's no rest for the wicked and birthdays are no different! So, it's kind of like every other day in that sense, still have to repair this body.

---

sexual relationships. It is not uncommon for survivors' friends to experience difficulty adjusting to how the disability has affected the relationship. Also, friends often feel pushed out by family, children and partners, because it can feel as though the relationship that they have with the survivor is seen as secondary.

[37] I used to tell myself that my memory was 'just for a day', but now I realise that that is senseless: not all memory is the same. Even just dividing memories into long-term and short-term is excessively crude. Memories formed about autobiographical events, involving strong emotions are, unsurprisingly, stronger than memories of mundane details. Memories involving multiple sensory associations are stored more strongly than ones which rely on sound alone. Procedural memories, such as how to drive or of a routine task, tend to remain even after details of the autobiographical event fades.

[38] I genuinely did not know how old I was. I could tell you I was in my mid-20s. But, even if I did remember what year it was, I would be unable to do the mental arithmetic.

I got an email from Ben saying Kate and Fran are coming up this evening too. And my parents and Ben's parents are all going to be here. Then Ben's coming later and we've got the flat. So we'll be hosting a bit of a rave in there by the sound of it!

***

Wednesday 20th May 2009

Last night when Ben got here we went to get the keys for the flat, but they wouldn't let us have them! They said that a patient's not allowed to have the flat once they're allowed to go home at the weekend. So they wouldn't let us have it. Ben told them how it was my birthday and we'd booked the flat especially as a treat. Anyway, because they took pity on us, they let us have an impromptu visit home, which was even better. So last night I got to be at home with my Ben, which was the best birthday present ever.

But what have I done today, apart from basking in Ben's birthday love? Oh, it was mildly exciting... I had some medical students come to see me, the real life specimen of a diffuse axonal injury. I was in physio and I quite like it when I'm a wonder of science [39] It's a bit of a pathetic thing to brag about, but that doesn't stop me: "I've been in a coma for over a month, what have you done?"

***

Friday 22nd May 2009

Had OT today. It's quite sweet: they have a little children's cook book, which the patients are supposed to use. [40] I made some cake.

Then I had psychology. Suzy talked me through the results of my cognitive assessment thing. She always said how I did compared with the average. I asked her "the average of who?" She knows I went to Cambridge, so I said "not average when compared to the average Cambridge graduate." She didn't say it explicitly (they never do), but she was kind of saying "the old Faiza is dead, don't look down your nose at 'average'." I should just be delighted with how far I've got, by the sound of it. Maybe that's why they're always praising me.

---

[39] I have since discovered that a Diffuse Axonal injury is one of the most common head injuries in the developed world today, so I was not really the "wonder of science" that I thought myself to be.

[40] Children's cook books were chosen especially for use by the OT department, because the recipes were both easy to follow and written in simple English, making them accessible to neuro patients. Also, the suggested times would make allowances for the cookery skills of children. In the OCE the suggested times made allowances for patients' disabilities.

Anyway, I didn't even manage average on all areas. I guess this is what Najma means when she says "you're still not the old Faiza."

I do kind of remember the assessment exercises. It's a bit worrying that she could pick this up on the phone to me. I can't even console myself that the only thing this head injury has knocked out of my head is the ability to do those weird cognitive exercises. But it looks like it's even stuff that comes up being chatty with my best friend. But what I can't figure out is why no one ever says it to me. They're all being too kind. Or maybe they just can't tell. Maybe Najma's smart enough to pick up on it and everyone else is just too thick to see it.

And they were all quite babyish exercises. When I said this to Ben he pointed out that "they couldn't have been THAT easy if you got them wrong." But they were easy. I don't know.

Then in the evening Gemma came to visit. She said she was up in Reading. When she saw me she was so happy to see me walking! I was a bit freaked out by all this and told her that I've been walking for ages now. I can't remember how crippled I was the last time she came.

I'm looking forward to tomorrow. I managed to decipher Ben's handwriting on my on my calendar for tomorrow, saying that it's my "re-birthday party with friends". I think I'm allowed to go home for it.

***

Saturday 23rd May 2009

I came home yesterday. The OCE are quite cool about it all. They often say to me that patients like to be able to go home and it also helps people to settle back into everyday life. They keep going on about "re-introducing life" as this whole process. I think they just make a big deal out of it, because people like to make a meal out of everything. I guess some people do have more to deal with. My roommate has a baby or toddler. All I have is Ben. So it sounds like bullshit.

It sounds like I'm going to have quite a big birthday party. It's quite sweet that Ben's been calling it my "re-birthday party" in the invitations. I guess it must have been a big thing for him. He's made it "bring a dish", so we have quite limited stuff to do. I think he said his mum cleaned up our house before the OTs came round to check it was cripple-proof.

***

I continued to stay at the OCE throughout June. I was allowed home at weekends. During the week friends would come to see me. This was quite a nice time, but when I mention that to people they tend not to share my point of view.

I learned to walk without any aids, but a few months after discharge I bought a walking stick to act as a sign to the man in the street that I had 'the invisible disability'. Even though we all like to think that we live in a modern, forward thinking society, where people don't judge on appearances, I would be treated differently with the stick. This was, after all, why I carried it. Maybe it was simply because with it, I felt as though I could ask for allowances to be made.

So I began to grow resentful of wheelchair users, because they hogged the disabled identity. "If they'd only taught me to control my wheelchair, then I could be as independent as one of them!" They'd wheel along in them faster than I could walk, and could therefore cram their day fuller (more like how the old Faiza used to).

Both Ben and I lived in the space between the disabled and able-bodied worlds. My brain just could not compute what was wrong with it. Ben, on the other hand, was in denial, but still had to inhabit the disabled world with me. He worked hard to maintain the appearance that everything was normal. I really thought it was.

Generally the OCE worked to ensure that there were no major hiccups with returning back to my life. They managed all the wider circumstances that their experience had taught them happens at this stage. In fact, they managed it all so well that, helped by my lack of insight, I had no idea that anything was wrong. In fact, I would just get annoyed with them talking about the "long process of gradual adjustment".

As my functioning improved, I became more aware of the different aspects of my rehabilitation. Rather than watching the grown-ups mend my body, I started to play a more active role in my treatment. Katy [my physiotherapist] made me a splint that I was meant to have on for 4 hours a night. I couldn't go to the toilet while it was on, so I grew suspicious after noticing that whenever I called the nurse in the night to take me to the toilet I never had a splint on. I became convinced that it just sat in the corner of the room having not been touched all night. I'm sure many people preferred it when I was more docile...

People often feel that patients with neurological disorders "only remember what they want to" and just function for "what suits them". I could not problem solve and had difficulty initiating tasks. In my diary below, I describe the ludicrously elaborate method that I used to "catch the nurses out".

Yes, I could only problem solve "when it suited me". But, on the other hand, I was more motivated because it was in my interests (which can have enormous effects on person's cognitive abilities). For the able-brained reader all I can say is that it's sod's law!

***

Monday 6th July 2009

... I caught the nurses out! Last night I put a hair band on top of my splint to see if they were actually coming in to do it in the night. Then when I looked in the morning it was still there, untouched! They thought they could get away with it, and didn't think I could have hard evidence to prove them wrong, but I came up with a system. Anyway, I told Katy [my physiotherapist] this morning about it and she said she'd talk to the nursing team about it. Patients 1 - Nurses 0.

Wednesday 8th July 2009

... Then, in physio today I told her about the whole splint thing and she said she'd chase it up with the head nurse, so we'll see. They'll have to stop pretending about it now if nothing else. An apology or an admission of guilt is probably too much to ask for, but I just want the splint done. It's supposed to get me better.

Then I asked her about my bladder problems. I said I know that it's not really her job, but it's all part of the body. I wanted to train up my bladder. She suggested some exercises. Let's see if they work. [41]

***

Thursday 9th July 2009

Had physio today and she told me why the nurses didn't put my splint on. They said that I'd refuse to have it put on and that I must have forgotten! Can you believe that? They often grumble about how patients are "being difficult" and blame it on whatever's wrong with them. I guess they can pull the "able brained" card on me.

It's so annoying that they can just say that anything they don't like is "because of the patient's condition". Why can't someone just be annoying by birth? And, God forbid, why can't a paid member of staff be the uptight one, who doesn't know how to take what the cripple said as a joke? And this memory thing is quite frustrating because I can't remember "refusing" to have my splint put on.

---

[41] To help "train my bladder", the physiotherapist suggested some pelvic floor exercises that were designed for patients who have restricted mobility. These helped to strengthen the abdominal muscles that apply pressure on the bladder when I needed to empty it when on the toilet. As well as regaining neurological control of my urinary sphincter muscles, I had to adjust to removal of a catheter that I was reliant on when unconscious.

Anyway they've come up with this new way of doing it: putting the responsibility on me a bit more now[42]. I've put the splint on top of my pyjamas so that I keep up my side of the bargain...

***

The rest of July passed by for me as an in-patient at the OCE. I went home at weekends and some nights a week. Even though my memory was better, I still can't remember much of this time either.

On July 28th 2009, Leonard Cohen was playing at Weybridge in Surrey, about 15 minutes from Ben's parents' house. Ben is a massive fan and bought tickets for both of us, so that we could go and be a normal couple when I was on "weekend leave". We stayed at his parents, and an hour before we were due to leave I started feeling really tired – or to use OT language, 'was struck down with fatigue'. I went up to have a nap (or rather, to lie down with my eyes shut, feeling guilty about how affected Ben would say that I appeared). So he brewed me a strong cup of coffee and I drank it, thinking how coffee never wakes me up.

But it did. Ben says that he was amazed to see such a fundamental shift in my being. He said it was as if I had never crashed the car; even my voice lost its slur. I did feel a bit brighter, I'll give him that.

My discharge date from the OCE was 31st July 2009. Then a few weekends after that I had a 'coming out party' (pun very much intended). This was a gathering of my closest friends. I enjoyed it: I love playing the host. But the house had been primarily under Ben's care since my car crash and it needed cleaning up.

I set aside the week before it to do just this. It was just like one of the cognitive exercises that the OTs gave me. Step one: write out a list of all the jobs. Step two: organise this into a timetable, taking care to pace myself, ensuring that I allowed enough time to complete each step. Step three: clean house ready to present it to the world.

---

[42] It was agreed that I would call the nurses on the buzzer before I went to bed to ask them to help me put it on. Then the same nurse would come 4 hours later, at 2 o'clock in the morning, to remove it as I slept. This system helped me to take greater responsibility for my own rehabilitation, in preparation for discharge.

Playing the host at my coming out party. We had to hold it in the day, after having
been advised that this would be wiser, since I do not function well at night.

4   Synapses

Physiotherapy had already started when I was in the JR. My concentration had been affected by the brain injury, and being asked to perform a series of peculiar tasks in unfamiliar surroundings for strangers did not help. But when Ben came with me, I would be calmer and manage to stay focussed.

Focus was essential because the goals of neuro-rehab can only be achieved through brain reprogramming. During a head injury, the brain has been struck, shaken violently or starved of oxygen. Neurones (brain cells) are destroyed.

Some of the neurones that were destroyed were the ones that helped access memories. Their death resulted in amnesia. Others were the neurones which helped the brain to interpret the signals it received from its senses. I had 'double vision', because my brain could not integrate the images it was receiving from its two eyes.

So, in neuro-rehab, physiotherapists perform exercises, which help the patient to "remember how to walk" by taking advantage of the brain's 'neuroplasticity'. As we learn something new (a physical skill or a make memory) the brain's neurones form new pathways, which have the skill programmed into them. In a brain injury the existing pathways have been destroyed and the brain has to navigate a new path, avoiding the damaged nerves.

Some cells have died. They will never come back to life. Neuroplasticity means that the skill has been lost; but it can be re-learnt.

**

Rachel, my physiotherapist, came to collect me from the ward. As usual she wheeled me over to the "gym". This session I was going to practice gripping. Or rather we were going to practice gripping. Apart from physically attending the session, there was not much I could do. But my brain was working very hard.chel put a light plastic cup in my hand and asked me to grip it. I couldn't. But the important thing was that I <u>thought</u> that I could, and closed my hand. While I was busy sending messages through my neurones, Rachel would do the hard work and push on my fingers to fool my brain into thinking that the message had worked. In this way, my brain would learn what gripping feels like and connections would be made. So next time we did this, Rachel could get away with doing 99% of the work, because I would do the remaining 1% myself.

Learning to grip was one of the more advanced physio exercises. While I was still in my coma (with a GCS of 5[43]), sitting upright in my wheelchair was seen as physiotherapy. Every day, I needed to spend 3 hours in my wheelchair. It was the sort of wheelchair given only to the severely disabled, who have difficulty supporting their own body weight. At this stage my neck was not strong enough to hold my head upright, and it just used to flop onto my chest or shoulders.

Ben did not feel that the physiotherapists were doing enough to help with this, and he often proudly recounts his innovation of supporting my head with a travel pillow that he had borrowed from his parents. I am told how this helped to hold my head in an upright position so that the neck muscles could get stronger, instead of just wasting away, with my head resting on its side.

As I made progress, physiotherapy sessions helped my body get used to being vertical. When I first got to the gym Rachel would strap me onto a table (the tilt table). After I had acclimatised, the table would be tilted to a more vertical position. Once "upright" (at first I would only be able to withstand 80°), Rachel would make what she called postural adjustments, to get my muscles used to holding my weight in the right way again.

Ben explains to me how the amount of physio I was getting was probably determined by cost rather than any medical judgement about fatigue. He did not feel that I was receiving the optimal amount of physiotherapy, so he asked Rachel for some additional exercises that he could do with me. She explained to him how a major hurdle I would face if I got better enough to walk, would be that my muscles would be so stiff that I would barely be able to move – so she gave us some stretches for my calf.

If I ever got better enough to walk, these exercises would make movement easier. When the brain is unable to send messages to the legs, there is a tendency for the toes to end up pointing downwards. The stretches helped to get my feet pointing in the right direction again, which is somewhat essential for walking!

---

[43] GCS refers to the Glasgow Coma Scale, a scale which runs from 3 to 15 and is used to measure the depth of a coma. I talk about this more thoroughly in chapter 6.

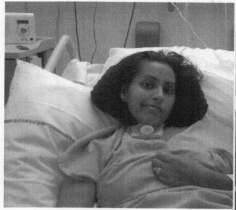 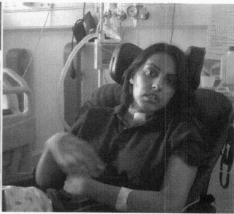

This, I am told, is a really good photo of me. I was actually able to smile (albeit asymmetrically) and look into the camera. The blue cushion behind my head is Ben's neck-supporting travel pillow.

In this photograph you can see that I am sitting on the hoist that would be used to "transfer" me from the bed to the chair. My right hand is blurred because it would never stop shaking. My left arm was feared paralysed.

Once I no longer needed to be attached to a machine, I was able to go off the ward for an hour or so during the day. However, motion was something that the body was not used to, so I would get travel sick on the smallest of journeys. Even going down to the hospital canteen for a glass of juice was, at first, out of the question for this reason[44].

---

[44] I would always have juice rather than coffee, because I knew that caffeine was an ADH (anti-diuretic hormone) inhibiter. When I was studying GCSE biology, my brother, Naveed, was a fourth year medical student and I lapped up this sort of information in one of our many nerdy after-dinner conversations. This reinforced my school curriculum, where I was learning about the essential role of ADH in controlling the volume of urine a person produces. Even my damaged brain could deduce that I could not afford to mess about with my ADH when I wet the bed as often as I was told I did.

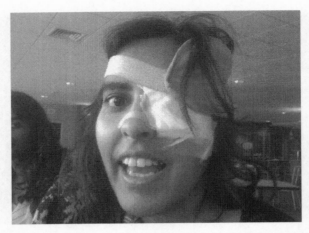

This photograph is a later one, when I could withstand being wheeled down to the hospital canteen. I had one eye covered. There was nothing wrong with it: this was to help me with the double vision. The hospital's latest policy was to not use eye patches, but one of the nurses dug out some old ones and gave them to Ben. However, since he only had five, they had to be carefully rationed. (In fact they were so well rationed that we still have one left.) To conserve eye patches, Ben's make-shift solution was to tape a bandage over one of my eyes, leaving me looking like some kind of deranged pirate girl. In this photo I have a definite look of mania, which is typical of the inability to control emotion associated with damage to the frontal lobes.

***

Towards the end of my time in the JR, I felt bored and frustrated. Ben used to cheer me up by constantly reassuring me that "we" would be going to another hospital, which would be full of exciting activities for me. He told me that this would be a rehabilitation centre. I felt quite excited because I knew that rehab was where the likes of Amy Winehouse and Pete Doherty[45] had been.

Because I had lost over a year of memories and forming new ones was difficult, I had no idea what the date was. At first, I could not even tell you what year it was, let alone the month or day. So, Ben brought in a calendar that I had on my wall. He wrote on in large colourful letters "going to the OCE ☺" on Wednesday the 15th of April 2009.

---

[45] I had vivid memories of Pete Doherty and Amy Winehouse's relationship, because it seemed to be what the kids at school were always talking about in 2007, when my memories started to fade away.

The 'Oxford Centre for Enablement' was over the road from the JR. At the time, I was unable to grasp that a centre for enableMENT was different from calling it a centre for the enablED. I thought that it had been called this through some absurdly PC use of positive language, similar to the way that short people would be referred to as 'vertically challenged'. People always seemed to be doing their upmost to avoid calling a spade a spade, or a cripple a cripple.

Even though I was unable to pick up on subtler aspects of communication, I was all too aware how people insisted on claiming that I'm not disabled, even though I was wheelchair-bound (and not just a normal wheelchair – a proper cripple's wheelchair). "They're all disabled in there, so why do they have to insist that they're enabled?" Before my time there started, and even for my first few weeks there, I always called it the 'Oxford Centre For Disablement'.

It was only much later that my cognitive ability had developed enough to give me the imagination to name it the "Oxford Cripple Establishment".

5 Cognition of Disability

By the time I had arrived at the OCE, I knew I had memory problems because people always seemed to be mentioning events of which I had no memory. I would love to claim that the reason I believed them is that at heart I am a kind and trusting individual (perhaps with the patience of a Saint). The reality, however, is somewhat less dignified. Often people would recall a joke that I had made in the past. This would leave me paralysed, laughing with emotional lability[46] and I would have no choice but to think, "It's *so* funny, only *I* could have authored that one." I was forced to conclude that I must have sort of memory problem.

When I woke up in the mornings I would often switch on radio 4. There was something about the tum-tee-tum of the Received Pronunciation voices that would calm my hectic mind in a way that music stations never could. At the time I was unable to make sense of exactly why, but now it seems alarmingly obvious: music requires the listener to process several streams simultaneously, whereas listening to speech requires only processing a single element at any instant.

I would probably be unable to follow most of it[47], but was always blissfully unaware of that, too busy priding myself on how typically intellectual and middle class I was, listening to Radio 4. All my fellow inmates at the rehab centre would be listening to was Kiss FM!

---

[46] Emotional lability is generally associated with damage to the pre-frontal cortex of the brain. The exact emotions that are exhibited can vary, but common examples include the survivor being overcome by fits of laughter or outbursts of anger.

Its causes can be diverse, but common reasons are brain trauma, dementia or stroke.

[47] I was unable to follow the involved discussions on Radio 4 probably because of how my memory problems and slower processing speed combined to reduce concentration.

One morning I happened to tune into a report on an initiative being conducted in Hackney. My ears pricked up because it was a pet subject of mine: gifted children's education. The Local Education Authority (LEA) was working with its primary schools to help prepare their most able students for their Key Stage 2 SATs. In order to give the listener a window into what the LEA were doing, the radio played one of the mental arithmetic tapes that they would play the students. The questions sounded quite easy and I played along, doing the sums in my head, writing down my answers to compensate for the memory problems, which I knew I had. Then when they read out the answers I had got all but one of them wrong. I came to the confused conclusion that, "There must be something wrong."

***

I had woken up from a coma into a land where people spoke a language of peculiar medicalised terminology to describe the likes of me. In my skull looped a track of doctors' and therapists' voices and I began to recall the words "cognitive impairments", which they all used when talking about my "head injury". It gradually dawned on me that the head contains a very important organ, the brain. "But", I told myself, "at least I'm not brain damaged."

I did, however, begin to accept the fact that something was wrong with the way that I thought. But I still felt the same. I had no idea what to make of this. The activities I did in my occupational therapy sessions seemed to have some weird agenda all of their own. I found the cooking sessions the most frustrating, because I was a good cook (wasn't I?), but the OTs seemed to be obsessed with doing everything in an excessively laboured way: they seemed to spend more time ordering the tasks, rather than actually doing them[48]. They would get out ALL the ingredients and do ALL the preparation BEFORE getting the pan hot. All they would ever let me do were boring recipes (or worse still, make a cake from a 'just add water' pack).

"Why won't they believe me when I tell them I'm a really good cook?" I constructed my own theories about how they wanted to clock off early for lunch, and tried little tactics to avoid a patient session which was due to finish around our 12:15 lunch time.

***

---

[48] In my Occupational Therapy cooking sessions, the ordering and sequencing of tasks was always emphasised, because they are key to helping head injury survivors tackle their impaired 'executive functioning'. Allocation of resources and the sequencing of tasks are key things to focus on.

Ben has told me about an incident that we (well, I) referred to as "the reciprocating bed confusion". I have no memory of this occasion, which is a crude indicator of how deeply I was affected by the brain damage. It seems I was never able to grasp the fact that no one was claiming that the mattress reciprocated (flipped upside-down), but I had already given this incident that title and re-naming it would be too arduous a task.

In order to help make me feel more at home, Ben used to replace the hospital's white, flat bed sheets with our own coloured, fitted sheets that he had brought in from home. Unfortunately, our own special sheets didn't fit on the hospital beds. Unsurprisingly, hospital furniture is not designed to accommodate patients' individual bed linen requirements, so our fitted bed sheet would not remain secured unless the mattress lay flat. One of the elasticated fittings would always come away to leave a corner exposed.

One afternoon, I raised my bed head on one of these orthopaedic beds that Ben had personalised in this way.

"I can't fit this properly," I said to Daddy, "Can you pull it on, because you've got more strength?"

"Nay," he said to me, before explaining to me that the weakness in my arm was not the problem. It was the fact that these sheets were never designed for specialist hospital orthopaedic beds. Then, later on, when Ben came to the hospital to visit, I seized the opportunity to appeal to his reasonable nature to use his able body to fit the sheet for me: I had already spent all day in the distressing presence of this loosely fitting sheet. But, when he arrived he echoed my father's explanation that it was not my physical impairments that affected my inability to fit the sheet, but the fact that the sheet just would not fit.

"Ukh! That's what my dad said," I shouted out, feeling deeply frustrated at how no-one, not even Ben, could appreciate the simple fact that if you just pulled a bit harder it would lie flat.

***

When I was discharged from hospital I did not really understand why people would advise me to wait before returning to work. I knew that I had been in hospital for 6 months, so I was happy that it stood to reason that I should have a similar amount of time off work, "resting at home". My discharge was in the summer, so I knew that, because of the way the school year worked out, I would have to wait, annoyingly, until September of the following year. I simply told myself "such is life", hoping to use my time off sick to indulge in some creative activities.

I imagined that I would use my time to complete arty projects around the house, such as paintings and mosaics. But I was able to initiate only a handful of the projects that I should have done, because my productivity paled in comparison with "old Faiza's" vitality. My reduced insight protected me from appreciating just how dreadful the situation really was.

A lot of the time I was quite tired (or struck down with 'fatigue', as it was referred to by therapists and authors of head injury advice literature[49]). Most afternoons I had to retire to bed after an exhausting day of supporting my own neck. One time I asked Ben to lie with me and 'settle me in', then after a few moments he wished me, "Good night". But before he left I asked him to position the pillow in a position that I would find more comfortable.

I asked, several times, for the position of the pillow to be changed in quite a specific way so that it could better support my head. Ben has described this time to me since, recounting how he struggled to extricate himself from my confused and dysarthritic[50] ramblings. After a good few minutes of listening to how it was all his fault that he could not understand the instructions that I had explained so fully, he escaped my clutches and went to zone out and veg on his PlayStation.

Because he had not understood what I was talking about, it struck me that perhaps I should have expressed myself more clearly. So I lay awake racking my brain for a clearer description of what I had failed to communicate. If I used the most precise language I could, then he could no longer say it was my fault for being unclear. I woke myself up and recorded my instructions onto my Dictaphone.[51]

Being a nerd at heart, the words that I came up with were incomprehensibly precise to the layperson. Then, after about half an hour, Ben returned and I handed it to him. When he pressed play my slurred voice ordered him to, "Translate the

---

[49] The fatigue that neurological patients suffer from is different from the tiredness that most people experience: it is affected neurological functioning. Common effects can be slurred speech, affected thinking and a lack of emotional control. It is a nearly universal complaint of people with head injuries and is part of post-concussion syndrome (or PCS) that can occur for years after a traumatic brain injury.

[50] Dysarthria is a neurological impairment due to damage in the central or peripheral nervous system. It may result in weakness or paralysis of the lips and tongue. For me, the result was slurred speech caused by a lack of coordination of the motor-speech system. These effects hindered the control that I had over my tongue, throat, lips and lungs.

[51] Samantha, one of the few friends from Summertown College who I could remember, had bought me a Dictaphone, to help me deal with my memory problems. I kept it on my bedside table to record things which occurred to me in the night.

pillow by minus one and a half pillows along an axis parallel to the head board." What could be clearer than that?

He claims that this is what he did. Somewhat conveniently, I only have a very vague memory of this whole incident, so I cannot explain how what he was doing was different.

***

Headway is a charity that was set up in 1979 by a network of carers for their brain injured children. Now it supports all people affected by head injuries, not just infants. They have been a source of constant strength and emotional support for us. After I had been home for a few months, Nicki Holland, their volunteer coordinator at the Oxford branch, visited me. She came to discuss what voluntary work I might be able to do. When she came around for a visit she noticed some of the pots that I had mosaiced and suggested that I come to their day centre and teach mosaic classes to some of their members.

The first thing that we would need to do is ensure that I was comfortable getting myself there. She did a few trial runs with me when I could annotate a map with my own notes, so that I could successfully transfer buses to make it to their day centre independently.

In the autumn after I had been discharged, we were on one of our trial runs to the day centre and we got on a bus from Oxford. I was incredibly annoyed with a man who was sitting in the disabled seat even though he was obviously not disabled. He wore jeans, had short brown hair, and looked like a healthy, young man in his early twenties. He had placed his bag on one double seat and sat with his legs apart casually taking up the other double seat. He had occupied all four disabled seats: forcing me and Nicki to walk further down into the bus to find some other available seats.

I was outraged. He did not look disabled, but having the 'invisible disability' myself, I knew that looks could be deceiving. After we had sat down I asked him, "Are you disabled?"

"No. But if a disabled person gets on, I'd move."

I exchanged some disapproving glances with Nicki, who in retrospect, must have been in a bit of an awkward position: an innocent member of the public, whilst not behaving with upmost consideration, probably did not deserve to be aggressively interrogated by a random headcase.

It was only about a full year later that I was able to reflect on this and appreciate what had happened: I think I was convinced that he was breaking some kind of apartheid. I was aware that disabled people had separate wheelchair accessible toilets, allotted seats on public transport and even their own parking spaces. I knew that these things were meant to be for the disabled person's benefit, but we all know how that was just what they said: they had to hide their real motives. I thought what they were really designed for was to keep us crips apart from the able-bodied population. They presumably did not want to become tainted by our toxicity. I was a law-abiding citizen before the car crash and I wanted to stay one. I was in the same world; the only difference was that now I was on the other side of the cripple fence.

Often friends and relatives would reassure me that "you're not properly disabled", reacting to my own feelings of worthlessness. I knew that I was disabled, because I had been given a disabled parking badge and the Department for Work and Pensions (DWP) paid me disability living allowance (and I knew that the DWP never gives good money away without reason).

I soon came to appreciate that if I accepted the benefits and parking spaces then I should accept the stipulation of this apartheid. I found it upsetting that this man would not respect society's simple rules on the way that this segregation was organised.

***

Then in the summer of 2010 I attended a course run for a dozen or so people who had suffered head injuries and had been affected cognitively. Most of the other patients were at least a generation older than I was, but there were a couple of patients who were studying at a sixth form college. It was a nice group. We exchanged details of our injuries. I think we all enjoyed having a place where this was not taboo. We could be nosy and openly ask each other, "So, what happened to you?", "Which hospital were you in?" or "What scans have you had?"

I was really excited about attending this cognitive rehabilitation group (CRG) because I imagined that it would be like an exciting university module. The nerd in me revelled in the opportunity to learn about the structure of the brain and how its functioning can be affected by damage to its cells. But when I started at the group, it dawned on me that it was going to be far more practical than that: patients were encouraged to share their experiences, and were taught about strategies that could be used to manage their difficulties more effectively. References to the anatomy of the brain were minimal.

It is hard for me to write about this without mentioning the fact that I was quite annoyed by the department of psychology's approach to teaching: they seemed to have no understanding of the psychology of education. I was always taught that "a child is not a vase to be filled, but a fire to be lit." In other words, lessons tend to be dull and unsuccessful if you see yourself as 'the expert' whose job is to transfer knowledge from your enlightened brain into the students' empty heads. I have come to believe that children (or students of any age) learn best when asked to actively construct knowledge using engaging learning activities.

Delicate handling was definitely needed when asking a series of experts to teach a room full of brain-damaged cripples the best ways to deal with their own cognitive impairments. It could have left patients worried about being seen as stupid. The chance of this happening would only be increased if the students were taught about the brain by drawing pictures in pairs or playing games together. I suspect that this might explain why the psychologists chose to impart knowledge through the medium of bullet-pointed powerpoint slides. Or maybe they just knew that teaching with constructivist exercises is a nightmare to plan and that 'teaching from the front' is a lot less hassle.

One especially useful thing that the classes did teach me concerned relaxation. We learned about how often head injury victims can have difficulty relaxing[52], and we were talked through some breathing and visualisation exercises. After this I began to concentrate on my inhalations and exhalations when in bed. This seemed to cure my sleep problems.

Of course, we cannot claim that this overnight transformation was solely a result of the relaxation exercises that I learnt at CRG. It could have been that the brain managed to rewire itself to work around the damaged cells that used to let me relax. Or other changes in my life could have had psychological effects and relieved the tension I felt. But I still use the strategies to help me unwind before I fall asleep, by focussing my mind.

The best thing about the group was the chance to meet other people who were living with cognitive impairments. One of the people who most stands out in my memory of the group is a woman; let's call her Susan. Susan had suffered a head injury after her brain was starved of oxygen during a routine operation. We spoke every week about how we were doing. I have to confess, I found her quite difficult to talk to. She was always kind and well-intentioned, but I started to get a sense of what people meant when they spoke about 'a difficult head injury patient'.

---

[52] Often head injury survivors suffer from anxiety, which is why this part of the workshop looked at relaxation and we benefited from being taught relaxation methods. As well as a lengthy process of adjustment to affected cognitive functioning, damage to the pineal gland has been associated with feelings of anxiety and depression.

I have come to understand that the reason why people never elaborated on the meaning of 'being difficult', was not because they were protecting me from the truth, it was probably because there are no words that can really pin it down. The non-verbal communication that occurs between two people has been affected, so their contact becomes less intuitive. And also, in a way that is similar to autistic people, head injury survivors can have an impaired *theory of mind*[53], making it harder for them to take another person's perspective. This is probably why, after a head injury, we can have difficulties with relationships. People might be unable to find a new partner; their marriage may not survive the tension it has to withstand; or perhaps a parent-child relationship might buckle under emotional pressure.

Susan talked about her experiences in hospital and how she had become annoyed with the doctors who blamed her 'difficult behaviour' on the head injury. They never considered that she had not been in this overwhelmingly frustrating situation before, so how could they blame her behaviour on the injury itself? Was it the complex situation of the head injury or neurological damage that was causing the 'difficult behaviour'? Or as I helpfully added to the conversation: "They don't know how you would have acted if this had happened before your operation. Maybe you've always been this annoying?"

One week during a discussion, one man told the group about a particular difficulty his cognitive impairments had landed him in: when trying to dispose of some waste food when the kitchen bin was full, he flushed it down the toilet, causing hundreds of pounds worth of damage. He did not realise that this was not the correct way to dispose of unwanted food.

When I got home, I told Ben. He replied: "Like you".

"Like me! When?"

He told me that shortly after I had got out of hospital, we had afternoon tea with biscuits and I offered to clear it away. Ben found that I had indeed cleared it away: I had not washed up the cups, just placed them by the sink, and had cleared away the quarter plates from which we had eaten by putting them in the bin. He did not know what to say.

It kills me to be this unscientific, but basing my theory on a non-random sample size of two, the survey indicates that there is a cognitive impairment that stems from survivors' understanding of rubbish. We can fail to distinguish between its

---

[53] For a more involved discussion on this the more enthusiastic reader could have a look at 'Theory Of Mind Following Traumatic Brain Injury' in *Neuropsychologia*. 44 (2006) pp. 1623-1628.

different types: solid refuse; washing up; faecal matter (to be flushed), and so on. It all just comes under the general category of 'waste'. We can, therefore, fail to distinguish the various ways in which the rubbish should be disposed of – putting it in the bin, cleaning it up, flushing it down the loo.

The result is that they can be all be disposed of incorrectly, because they are all treated as generic 'waste'. They are all disposed of with no thought about the most appropriate method of disposal for that <u>particular</u> kind of waste. Therapists' language would phrase this as "a generally impaired ability to draw subtle distinctions in their daily lives". But that doesn't really capture the specific experiences of these head cases, and the specific ways in which their head injuries manifest themselves in day to day lives.

A few days later I talked to Ben about returning to work. Again, he did not know what to say.

6   Glasgow Coma Scale

From what I have come to understand, coming round from a coma is nothing like the waking up from a dream that Hollywood shows us. Even being in a coma is not a simple sleep (in the later stages the eyes are open to let the patient stare vacantly out). Its depth is measured on the Glasgow Coma Scale (or GCS). This rates the person on a score from 3 to 15. Patients gradually rise up through this as they 'wake up'.

The score is made up from three components: motor responses, verbal ability and eye functioning. At my worst I had a GCS of 3, the lowest of 1 for each of the three categories. I would joke about how this was one of my worst ever exam results.

A score of three meant that I was silent (never made verbal responses), my eyes were shut and I had no response to pain. I am told how I ascended the scale painfully slowly. A week later I could make random moaning noises, extend my right arm, and open my eyes in response to pain. The doctors, however, still kept me under sedation to stop my brain from swelling and causing yet more damage.

Because the injury was to the microscopic neurones that make up the brain, no brain scan[54] would be able to pick out the damage. The only thing that pictures of my damaged brain could tell us was that I had a haematoma (blood clot) on the right side of the brain. It looked like it was dangerously close to the brain stem, which controls all the most basic bodily functions, such as control of the cardiovascular and respiratory systems.

I have been told that the lung infection I had (from inhaling some vomit after the car crash), began to escalate. The night of the 2nd of February 2009, was an important one. That night Ami, and I suspect everyone around me, prayed frantically all night in the ICU relatives' room. I managed to keep my heart beating through the night, but none of the doctors were really able to predict to what extent and in which ways my functioning would be affected.

---

[54] A functional MRI could have detected a lack of activity in the affected areas, but is not commonplace for this sort of treatment.

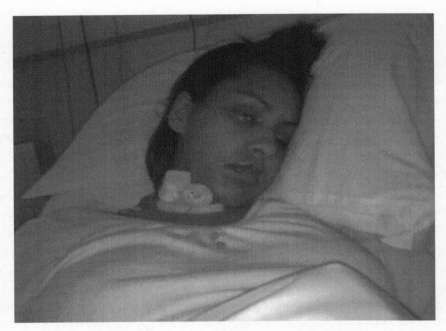

A family friend, Omar-Bhai[55], advised Ben to take these photos. Omar works as a doctor, and had seen people who woke up from a coma refusing to believe the stories that they were told about what happened to them: they have no memory of it, so it must be a lie. This is why Ben took these unflattering pictures of me linked up to a massive metal box, acting as my lungs.

Over a week after the car crash, the doctors decided to lift the sedation. My family watched me expectantly, hoping that I might miraculously wake up, just as people do in the movies. But I stayed in my coma. Over time, they began to appreciate that the root of my coma was not the drugs that the doctors had injected into my body, it was my damaged brain.

Another week later, when it looked like I would be in need of this machine for some time, the doctors made an incision across my neck in order to provide direct

---

[55] *Bhai* is the Urdu word for brother and because Omar Hussain is several years older than me, I always call him Omar *Bhai* (brother Omar) to demonstrate my respect for him. Technically I should call my brother "Naveed *Bhai*" because he is seven years older than me, but since the age of a seven I have conversed mainly in English with him, so I tend to just call him 'Naveed'. I fondly tell a story to my non-Pakistani friends about how once, when we were staying with relatives in Pakistan, the room was filled with raucous laughter when everyone was told that I call my brother by his name.

access to my windpipe and the ventilator's tube was inserted into it. I have since learned that this procedure is called a tracheostomy and the tube (and its associated scar) is called a trachey. Eventually, once my pneumonia had cleared and I had sufficient control over my diaphragm muscle, I was weaned off the ventilator and moved onto the neurosciences ward.

I continued to climb the GCS ladder and eventually reached a GCS of 9. Technically this meant I was no longer in a coma, but was barely human. A GCS of 9 meant that I had: an 'abnormal flexor response to pain' (I would indiscriminately move my body and/or limbs about if I had pain inflicted on me); 'inappropriate speech' (I was able to randomly shout out words, which although clearly articulated, were not able be part of any conversational exchanges); and an ability to open my eyes.

Until I had been weaned off the ventilator, the volume of my speech was virtually inaudible. To combat this Ben was shown by Rachel, my physiotherapist, how to cover it up by placing a clean finger over its opening. Of course, she would never condone such an action, because it would expose me to a minute risk of infection, but this is how Ben told me he would talk to me.

Even while I was in this state of total inertia, I was still given physiotherapy. This involved simple jobs, such as performing stretches on my body or putting a splint on my limbs. The splints helped to stop my muscles contorting my limbs into shapes which would not be good in the long run. Once I was moved onto the ward, Ben could supplement all this with his own additional physio routine. He would sit me up in a chair, get me to do 'sit ups' (sitting upright from slouching) and manually stretch my limbs out. All the while he would present this to me as tasks which "we" had to work on at in order to get better. Ben, because he did not want to dwell on the negatives, (and I, because of my reduced insight), did not really appreciate what this 'better' would look like.

I have virtually no memory of this time. I have been back to these places (the ward, ICU and the hospital canteen) when I have had other appointments at the John Radcliffe hospital. All that happens is that these places look vaguely familiar. Although that could be because of the generic otherworldly feel that inhabits all hospitals.

I was desperate to know more about this time and would ask Ben about it repeatedly. I think he just got sick of telling me.

"I've told you it all before. What do you want to know?"

"I don't know, just, what were things like?"

Everyone gave me their own different versions of this truth. So, Ben forwarded me a collection of emails that he sent out at the time. (Every few days he would send an email of my progress out to a collection of my friends and relatives.)

I'll let them tell my story. He claims that they are the best record of it.

7 Ben's Upd8s

I have included some of Ben's emails, because they are a well written and reliable summary of my time in the JR. I have kept them close to the originals.

Date: 6 February 2009 14:13
Subject: Update on Faiza
From: Benjamin Smith

Hi everyone,

This is just to update you all on Faiza's condition; apologies if I assume too much knowledge. Thank you all for your messages of support.

Also I don't know who has or hasn't been contacted about this, so I apologise if this is the first you've heard. Also if you notice I've missed anyone off then you're free to forward this email to them.

As you probably know, Faiza was in a car crash on Saturday morning and has serious head injuries. She's currently in neuro intensive care at the John Radcliffe hospital in Oxford.

Basically she's stable but still critical because of the pneumonia she's had. Tuesday night was a particularly perilous time, but she seems to have turned a little bit of a corner on Wednesday afternoon. She's very slowly getting better from it, but it's still critical.

With regards to her head injury, it's all a big unknown. They first thought she had a 'diffuse axonal injury'[56] (which is one of the worst head injuries you can get). We won't know for sure until she comes off the sedation that she's on at the moment.

---

[56] A diffuse axonal injury (DAI) is the diagnosis which I was in fact ultimately given. Axons are the long thread-like projections from the neurones, which make up the body of the brain. A DAI simply means that the neurones across the whole brain were affected – the injury is not localised, but 'diffused' across the whole web of axons. As the car ground to a halt my head was rapidly pushed back and forth. A common misconception is that the soft brain tissue collided with the hard walls of the skull, causing the neurones to die upon impact. What actually happens is that as the skull is shaken the soft brain tissue wobbles like

So at the moment we're waiting and hoping for her pneumonia to clear up, and hoping that it hasn't affected her head too badly (they interact because pneumonia starves the brain of oxygen if it's really bad).

If any of you do want to come and visit then you're very welcome to, but there is no compulsion on you to do so from me (it's obviously upsetting seeing Faiza as she is). I appreciate that your thoughts are with her in any event. If you do want to come up just give me a call/email. (Although my phone has decided to stop making any ringing sound, so I may not actually pick up - but leave a message.)

***

Ben continued to send out regular updates of this sort throughout February, to an ever-expanding list of people. He said he realised he'd created a monster when someone he was speaking to referred to it as the weekly 'bulletin'.

By the time the email pasted below was sent, I was off intensive care as my condition had stabilised. I was on the acute neurosciences ward, while outside the winter snow had begun to melt away.

This chapter does not contain every update Ben sent, so there are gaps between the emails reproduced here.

---

jelly. According to Ben, doctors used to say that the brain cells behave like snow in a snow shaker, and that the extremely delicate connections between the cells (the synapses) are severed by the violent shaking. Once dead, these connecting axons cannot spring back to life.

What then happens during the rehabilitation process is that the brain is simply 'rewired' to work around the dead cells. Some of the neurones that were being used to store information – such as memories, or functional things like how to walk – have died, and the information that they stored is lost. For example, some of the motor neurones may have died, which means that the brain's ability to innervate some kinds of muscle fibres will be reduced. The aim of the rehabilitation process is to re-form the electrical pathways between the remaining cells (or areas of the brain), through which information is stored. In this way, the brain is slowly helped to 'relearn' anything it has 'forgotten'. Rehabilitation does not, of course, involve interfering with the neural pathways directly; I did not need brain surgery to recover! The brain is always open to learning new things, so a lot of rehabilitation is about putting the brain in situations where it has to learn what it needs to re-form pathways. Exercises of any kind help neurones to store new information, and there is much in common between rehabilitation and other kinds of teaching and learning. The information in question could be anything from Newton's laws of motion, to how to manipulate the finger muscles. The difference is that rehabilitation is re-learning: this is why neurologists prefer to use the word rehabilitation rather than recovery, because the dead cells never come back to life, as they were before: the brain simply learns to work around them.

***

Date: 2 March 2009 14:19
Subject: Faiza: another update
From: Benjamin Smith

Hello everyone,

It is by now high time that I sent out another of these emails, so here we are.

Faiza is still on the neurological ward at the John Radcliffe. The easy way of measuring her progress is her coma score, which is now a 9. It has been 9 for most of the week, and briefly blipped to a 10 on Wednesday (but I think this might have been an anomaly). The difference now at 9 is that the movement in Faiza's limbs is now deemed to be more normal than before.

Faiza has, however, improved in some ways that are not measured on the scale.

First, she is almost certainly responding to instructions to blink her eyes. We have all seen this, including the seldom-present doctors and nurses. The first time Faiza did this was actually last Monday, but over the course of the week she has been doing it more consistently. Faiza now seems a bit more awake, and seems to be dipping less frequently into the deep unconsciousness that last week she was constantly flitting in and out of.

And what's more, we even seem to have detected hints of a half-smile. Again, we first noticed this about a week ago, but then it only seemed to appear when we'd actually done something to make Faiza smile! Now she seems to be able to do to command; I think this must be an improvement because it now involves a conscious intention on Faiza's part, rather than it just being a more visceral, bodily response. This would be consistent with the view that Faiza is spending less time in the hazy unconsciousness that she seemed to be in most of the time before.

Faiza is also dribbling quite a bit less than before, which renders useless my newly-learned skill of applying suction! I think this is a good thing because it means that she has more control over her mouth-muscles and is therefore able to manage her saliva herself. I also think Faiza has been responding when I have kissed her - but this is probably quite subjective so I would not set too much store by it!

In terms of Faiza's limb movements, she is basically just moving her right arm & right leg a bit more normally. She has been crossing her right leg over her left, and has been starting to move her arm at the shoulder. The most encouraging thing, though, has been that she can now start to grip a little bit. Whereas before Faiza had only just begun to move her right index finger, now she can move her thumb as well, and can also maintain a bit of tension in her other fingers.

She also seems to be aware of objects around her. On Saturday I decided to play her some music from my phone. I was holding the phone in front of her so she could see it, and low and behold a little hand crept up with its fingers waggling about trying to grab the phone! I helped her to grab it and Faiza held the phone for a good while. We also managed to get her to grab the phone to instruction yesterday, which is obviously a good sign.

Faiza seems sometimes to have quite a high level of awareness. Last night I was reading to her, and interrupted the flow to ask her if she actually wanted me to carry on reading. I said to blink if she wanted me to stop, and she blinked! If this is reliable then it seems to me to indicate that in addition to a basic cognitive awareness of the presence of objects, Faiza has emotions of some sort going on, and can even link these emotions to her experience of the world around her. Later on I put the hospital TV on for her and asked her to blink if she wanted me to take it away, and she blinked again.

Also I asked Faiza if her neck was hurting (the nurses had positioned the pillow quite awkwardly), and she blinked in response.

Faiza is now being fed through a tube that goes straight into her tummy (rather than through her nose as before). This is not that significant, except that i) it is a better way of feeding her, and ii) it means that the doctors expect Faiza to require a feeding tube for a significant amount of time.

Faiza is also being weaned off of her tracheostomy, and they are expecting to take it out at some point this week. Once it is taken out, we will be able to see if Faiza can make any speaking-noises.

I think that's all, so I'll just finish by reiterating my thanks for your emails and my appreciation of visitors. I should also say that I think visitors are probably good for Faiza, both because it lets her know that there are lots of people there for her, and because it helps to give her brain some sort of stimulation. The more the merrier![57]

---

[57] When I came out of hospital, I was taken aback by the various gifts that people had brought me. The most memorable one was aromatic bath oil. When I asked Ben why

Take care everyone,

Ben

Date: 17 March 2009 00:38
Subject: Faiza update
From: Benjamin Smith

Hello all,

It's that time again, so here we go with the news on Faiza.

This week Faiza's coma score does indicate a real change in her condition: as of last Thursday, she's a 14. This is really good news! The change since before is that Faiza has been speaking to us, even with the tracheostomy in. Also, the trache came out this morning, which is another piece of good news.

I will try to be logical in the way I divide the information up, so my apologies if this is a bit choppy.

To take the simplest thing first, the trache came out this morning because Faiza's neck is now strong and mobile enough to support her head without the risk of collapsing her airway. With the trache out, her voice has been more like a normal voice than a whisper.

In terms of her linguistic ability, Faiza is able at best to form full sentences, albeit basic ones. That's why her score is as high as 14. She seems basically to have bypassed all of the intervening stages in language development, presumably because she had the trache in, which made it very difficult for her to make murmuring-noises or to say isolated words. The next step up the coma ladder would be for Faiza no longer to be 'confused', which I think is defined in terms of things like knowing where she is, what date it is, and so on.

---

someone would buy bathing products for someone who was in a coma, he explained that it was so that he could open it for me and place it under my nose for me to smell. They didn't know for certain that I wasn't 'locked in', so any kind of stimulation might have been useful. At this time, no one was able to tell which of my senses I was able to use to access the environment. Quite often survivors' hearing and vision can be affected (they can still see and hear, but the brain cannot interpret the signals that it receives). My sense of smell was an avenue of sensory input that may have been worth exploiting. I now think this a good window into my family's concerns: they could not afford to leave any sense unexplored.

The story of Faiza's first post-accident sentence is a revealing one. We - by which I mean myself, Faiza's parents and my mum - were sitting around in Faiza's room at about 8 o'clock on Thursday evening, and Faiza seemed pretty groggy. The nurse asked in a rather grave tone if she could have a word with me outside. We went out of the room, and she asked me something relatively unimportant about Faiza's menstrual cycle. We then came back in and continued as before. Soon after, everyone left and I had some time alone with Faiza, whereupon she started trying to say something to me! Her words were almost indecipherable at first, but after literally about 30 attempts at interpreting what she was saying I repeated back to her, "What did the nurse want?" A relieved Faiza nodded back to me! I told her what it was and reassured her that it was nothing to worry about. Faiza then started to say a variety of other things to me, some of which we managed to decipher and some of which we didn't.

There are lots of interesting things to say about this, and I'll try to say some of them! First, Faiza asked an appropriate question in the form of a grammatically-correct sentence. The fact it was a sentence helped her up the coma scale, and more than that, it wasn't just gibberish - it made sense in the social context. Second, Faiza was aware that the nurse wanted to talk to me about *her*. She must be aware of what's going on conversationally, but more portentously she was aware of the nurse's *tone*. (I have read that tone is one of the subtler features of language, which people with head injuries tend sometimes to struggle with.) Third, Faiza waited until everyone else had left the room before she tried to ask me what the nurse had said. This means she must be aware of the different people around her, and made the decision to wait until she was alone with me before she tried to ask me the question. Fourth, Faiza has a definite self that exists through time, and must have some sort of short-term memory (at least). She must also have some form of attachment to me/her family (as opposed to the nurse, who she didn't ask the question), if not even some sense of her own privacy as opposed to the public authority of the doctors & nurses. And fifth, Faiza seemed to be sufficiently aware that she is ill for her to worry about it. She was definitely worried when she asked me the question, and it was this anxiety that prompted her to make what must have been an extraordinary effort to ask it.

So now we come to the downside of Faiza's increasing level of awareness: she seems to be increasingly aware of her situation. I related in my last email [not included here] how Faiza told me that she had been scared. This sense of anxiety on her part is probably present in her asking me about what the nurse had said to me, but it's definitely present in two other incidents. First, she told the nurse straight out yesterday that she was scared. I wasn't there, but the nurse told me about it later on; she didn't seem to appreciate the awful gravity of this. Second, when the speech and language therapist and I were talking with Faiza on Friday, Faiza asked, "When will they give me the all clear?" This was a horrible question to be asked. At the time I thought it implied that Faiza didn't realise that she was ill, and perhaps thought she was being detained unnecessarily. But now I think she was also trying to ask, "When will I get better?"

Saying that, Faiza doesn't give the impression of someone who is suffering terribly. She is half-delirious most of the time, and needs lots of sleep and rest. Most of the things that she says at the moment would come under the category of nonsense, and those that wouldn't are not as tortured as the incidents I've just mentioned. I have found comforting the thought, which I think is realistic, that she seems to experience doubt and anxiety for about the same amount of time during the day as we do. The rest of the time is spent day-dreaming (like us!) and sometimes interacting, but always within the cloudy context of her dreaminess.

To give you an idea of how Faiza is during the day, she spends most of the time either asleep or almost asleep. Of her awake time (which is roughly 20% of the time), most of it is spent just looking ahead in silence. Faiza only makes eye contact when you press her to, and only looks around the room when someone new comes in. She doesn't talk for the majority of the time, and when she does talk it's mostly nonsense. Today, for example, there were probably 2-4 periods of about 5 minutes each when we were able to 'converse' with Faiza.

Also, when Faiza does reply to questions, it is necessary to repeat them gently to her a few times; she takes lots of time to think, and sometimes she drifts off in the middle of her thought process. What I'm hoping to see over the next week or so would be a small increase in the amount of questions she manages to reply to, and more time spent deliriously awake rather than just staring ahead. I think Faiza will need lots and lots of sleep for quite a long time to come.

The other good thing is that Faiza's swallow has been strong enough for her to eat some pureed foods. On Thursday she tasted her first food for 6 weeks, which was some thickened ribena. The therapist called it a 'sorbet', and when she asked Faiza if she'd like some more, Faiza very endearingly said, "More sorbet please." I could have kissed her then! She has had some other smooth foods since, such as ice cream and mashed potato, and today we gave her some thickened hot chocolate. She said it wasn't very nice though!

This is really cool, and is potentially very significant from the point of view of Faiza's long-term quality of life. Now that the trache's out, we're hoping to start giving Faiza more foods over the coming few days. In time the plan would be to see how she copes with food that has lumps in it, and then eventually normal food - but at the moment this is still a very, very long way off.

Changing the subject to Faiza's more physical condition, she started a few days ago to move her left leg! This is really great news, as we thought it was going to be completely paralysed. And on Saturday, Faiza moved the fingers on her left hand by a millimetre or so, once or twice during the day. Then today, she moved her left hand at the wrist for the first time, again once or twice. The downside, though, is that the muscles in her left arm have become really tight, and they are considering putting it in plaster in order to hold it straight, and maybe even doing botox injections into the muscles to keep it in the right place.

The other change has been that Faiza has been moving around slightly less on her right hand side, which I think is a good thing because it means that more of her movement is done on purpose. We're not quite sure what the movement was before.

I think that's it. I should probably add some closing thoughts. These are obviously encouraging signs, but it's easy to get carried away with the fact that each week I'm able to report a list of improvements. The fact remains that Faiza has a very long way to go, and is still entirely dependent on carers for every aspect of her everyday life.

Finally, Faiza needs loads of sleep at the moment. Visitors are definitely appreciated, but I think now more than ever it's really important to let her rest when we see her. So if Faiza's sleeping when we come in, we should either go out of the room or just whisper. Her sleep is disrupted enough by the incongruous hospital routine (she is not allowed to sleep for longer than a few hours at a time, even at night), so we don't want to make things worse than they are already. Also we need to be restrained in asking Faiza to say and do things for us, as she is very easily tired out. Even setting aside her medical need for rest, she is in a horrible enough emotional situation as it is, without us disturbing even her restful time!

I should also say that the hospital don't allow anything nice like plants or flowers. We sneaked some into Faiza's room yesterday, but were told to remove them this morning!

OK, take care everyone, and thanks for all your good will. See you soon.

Ben

***

When re-reading these emails for this book, Ben commented to me that it is easy to get the impression that everything was quite alright and that I was OK really. For example, there is a paragraph above that talks about the foods that I ate, and what my response was to them. But really, all these foods were brought out to me by my family who were desperate for me to be normal, with zero input from me whatsoever. I never said if I did or did not like them – with the hot chocolate, for instance, Ben says I just refused to drink it by pressing my lips tight together, and then simply nodded when asked if it was horrible. The reality then was of a very brain-damaged person who was not really there for most of the time, and a family of loved-ones trying frantically to bring them back at all costs.

Around the end of March I began to struggle to come to terms with my disability, and my mood was another thing my family had to be concerned about. Here is an excerpt from an email Ben wrote to my brother:

Date: 25 March 2009 22:55
Subject: Faiza
To: Naveed Siddiqui
From: Benjamin Smith
  ...

I mentioned in my email that Faiza has been getting depressed: this has been totally confirmed today. The easiest way to put the point is that the nurse asked Faiza if she was OK, and Faiza said no. She then asked what the matter was, and Faiza said, "I'm depressed." I've asked them to prescribe some antidepressants for her, and they're doing that - but obviously they won't take effect for a few weeks. Another thing is that Faiza was talking a lot today about various people committing suicide: and then something about "Khadija", who I don't know anything about - Faiza said first that her sister and then that her friend was thinking of doing it.

Basically I asked Faiza if she thought that Khadija's friend should kill herself (my analysis is that this friend/sister might not exist (or might be Faiza), and was Faiza's way of thinking about what she herself wants to do), and she said "Yes", she should kill herself. I then asked Faiza if she was thinking about suicide herself, and she said "Yes, but..." and trailed off.

At least there was a but. Independently of how horrible all this is, it's affecting Faiza's recovery both in the sense that she has been doing less physio because she's seemingly so tired, and because she's not engaging with the world around her and is resting entirely in her internal, delirious world. It's almost impossible to prompt her without her just switching off and ignoring us...

Anyway, I hope you're OK, and sorry for writing another long email! My love to Erum & Humza.

Take care,

Ben

Ben had noticed that I was feeling very low. Here is an excerpt from what he wrote in his own diary a week earlier:

19/03/2009

As I write this, Faiza is in bed again, sleeping after the morning's exertions.

I received a phone call yesterday morning from Karen, Faiza's nurse for most of this week, informing me that Faiza had fallen out of bed. Thankfully she wasn't hurt, so I'm pleased that this is a sign that Faiza is beginning to regain her strength.

Also yesterday, Faiza ate her first post-accident meal. It was broccoli in a cheese sauce, served with carrots and mushy peas (the peas were an unsolicited extra!). She devoured about a quarter of it. I also brought in some grapes (Faiza had two), some strawberries (Faiza had 2 big ones) and some Philadelphia with some granary bread[58] (Faiza had very little of this). The nurse said that if Faiza continues to eat well, they'll be able to reduce the feed going through her PEG tube.

On entering Faiza's room this morning, I found her laying on her back <u>on the floor</u>, being attended to by a nurse. Apparently, Faiza had flung herself out of her wheelchair and the nurse had come just in time. This was in line with Dad's rather prescient prediction last week, and again we were lucky that Faiza was not hurt.

By coincidence, Faiza's nurse today is Juli (pronounced 'Khoolie'), a Spanish nurse who looked after her in ICU. It's nice to have some continuity with the nurses!

---

[58] Granary bread with Philadelphia might not sound appealing, but it was one of my favourite snacks. I would often have some after an exhausting day of being "Mrs Siddiqui".

And then just now (about 20 minutes ago), I was sitting with Faiza when she said to me that she wanted to "be more independent." She said she wanted to sit up, "at ninety degrees." I tried to help her with this, and it soon became clear that Faiza was also trying to stand up! I tried to help her a little, but she slid down the chair and I wasn't strong enough to pick her up. I called the nurse and we hoisted Faiza back into her bed.

Faiza seems very frustrated, but it is good that she is fighting. She is tough, and I'm glad that she's showing it. I will have to push the physios on Faiza's behalf to do more with her — perhaps some standing up?!

But at least she is sleeping peacefully now, tired out after all her naughty, but quite understandable, exertions.

***

For the next two months in the JR, I managed to get stronger. Ben's updates, in line with his concerns at the time, became much more focussed on my progress with the small achievable targets that I was set. So the last two emails, that I have included here, are focussed more on these. In the interest of the readers' sanity I cut out the more mundane details, such as the length of time I could perform particular physical feats for. So these are heavily edited versions of his e-mails:

Date: 24 March 2009 23:21
Subject: Update on Faiza
From: Benjamin Smith

Hello everyone,

First of all, I'm sorry for not writing this email earlier. I've been a bit busy this last week, and this is my first chance to write anything worth reading. I have pasted most of the text of this email from an update I sent today to the rehabilitation centre that Faiza is waiting to get into, so it's addressed to a doctor rather than to you guys. I hope you don't object to my sloth!

i) Faiza's legs. I said in my last email that Faiza had begun to move her previously paralysed left leg. This movement has continued to improve, and Faiza can now move the leg purposefully and to command.

ii) Faiza's arms. I said in my last email that Faiza had just begun to move her left arm. Faiza's elbow, however, is still pretty stiff, and I would say that she is still about 25 or so degrees away from the full 180 degrees of a straight arm. Faiza has been wearing an inflatable plastic cast around this arm for about an hour a day. [59]

iii) <u>Sitting & Standing</u>. Yesterday the Neuro SHO asked the physio why Faiza isn't allowed to start walking yet; in response, Rachel showed him the work Faiza has been doing in physio, where she is able to sit on the bench with light support for 5 or so minutes, and can sit bolt upright for around 5 seconds at a time.

Faiza fell out of bed last Wednesday, and on Thursday got out of her chair twice (she has been undoing her belt). [60] She told me on Thursday that she wants to "be more independent" and that she wants to stand up, which is what she was trying to do. I told her that the way to do this was to work hard in physio, and she seems to have responded accordingly - she has been working hard in physio (both with Rachel and with my supplementary 'physio') and has not fallen out again.

Faiza has regularly been sitting upright in her wheelchair, and on Thursday she told me that she wanted "to sit at 90 degrees." [61] She could do this on her own, but

---

[59] Ben fondly recalls a story about this plastic splint. He had written a series of letters for me, for one day when he imagined I would have recovered. He writes, "You were a bit sleepy, so I thought it would be a good time to put your arm splint on. You always hated having it on, so I thought that if you were sleeping (comatose) you might not suffer so much as it stretched out your stiff, non-cooperative arm muscles. He writes...

"It was like a giant children's swimming arm-band, transparent and nearly a metre long, and it took ages to put on. After about 10 minutes of fiddling, trying to get your entire arm into it and then blow it full of air, I finally succeeded. I thought I'd take a break while you wore it, so I went to get some tea or a can of coke. I felt guilty about leaving you, but there was no point just sitting there while you slept. And with the arm splint on at least something good would be happening, even if I wasn't there making sure you didn't take it off.

"When I returned about 30 minutes later, you were disoriented. You looked upset and confused, not to mention sleepy still. The splint was on the floor. I felt awful for having left you, and for you to have been abandoned while I forgot all about you, swigging my stupid coke and eating mars bars. But then you said, in the sweetest, most innocent voice that I think I have ever heard, "When I woke up, there was this big envelope on my arm, Ben." This might not sound like much, but the child-like purity of your voice, and your utter bewilderment about the purpose of this mysterious 'envelope', was enough to bring tears of joy and of sadness to my eyes."

[60] Ben thinks that this was a suicide attempt. For obvious reasons he did not consider it wise to include this detail in an email to the rehab centre he was working hard to get me admitted to.

[61] The jury's out over why I chose to describe my desire to sit upright as "sit[ting] at 90 degrees". Therapists would explain it as an impaired ability to appropriately tailor communication for the intended audience. Ben says that I could sense that people were having difficulty understanding the way I expressed my brain damaged thoughts, so I

could not stay there for long. Faiza has also been trying to sit upright in her bed, and has been able to sit supported on the side of the bed with her feet on the floor.

iv) <u>Toilet</u>. Faiza has been able to tell me when she needs to go to the toilet. In the middle of last week, she said she needed to wee (in spite of having the catheter in), and towards the end of the week she told me she needed to poo. Unfortunately she can't walk to a commode, and as there is no bed pan her only option is to do it in her pants and to let the nurses clean it up.[62]

v) <u>Eating & Drinking</u>. Faiza has now graduated from pureed foods onto the soft-most section of the menu. She has also been able to drink water, tea & hot chocolate. Faiza is able to hold the beaker or glass herself and to drink from it herself, and can also spoon some foods into her mouth herself. At first, Faiza showed an equal preference for sweet and savoury foods, but since the weekend Faiza has been choosing to eat only sweet foods like ice-cream. [63] Her diet is currently being supplemented by food put in through her PEG tube overnight.

It is worth pointing out, though, that Faiza has showed less interest in food over the last 3 or so days. I think she felt at first that we were distracting her from the task of getting better (by getting up, doing physio and so on) by feeding her childish foods.

---

overcompensated and phrased it in with an unnecessary mathematical clarity. I am not so generous and I know that there no escaping the fact that I am a nerd at heart. My damaged brain could not think outside of the bizarre mathematical language which I use to make sense of the world. So, to me it shows that deep down this is how I think of things.

[62] Like many patients recovering from this injury, I would have to poo onto whichever surface I happened to be at. At first my level of awareness was so low that I was little more than a shell, unaware even of my own existence, let alone the fact I'd pooed myself. Ben tells me that as time passed and I got better, I became aware that this was happening. One problem was that the nurses wouldn't always clean it up properly, and would sometimes miss a spot or two. This happened once when I was conscious enough to take in the fact that I was sitting in faeces. When I realised I was horror-stricken, panicked and cleaned my hands by smearing the poo up the wall next to the bed.

[63] An excessive desire for sweet food is associated with frontal lobe damage. My love for ice cream became such an established fact that Ami would frequently ask the catering staff if she could have any untouched ice creams off of patients' meal trays after lunch. I can only imagine that it must have been incredibly difficult for a mother to see her daughter in a state, where she was unable to indulge in the simplest of life's pleasures. Given that I had only been able to swallow for a matter of weeks, procuring ice creams for me must have acted as a coping mechanism for her. Ben fondly recounts a time when Ami returned so heavily laden with ice cream that I had three for myself with some left over the rest of the family (both Naveed and Ben were able to feast and enjoy).

vi) <u>Consciousness</u>. After telling me last Thursday that she wanted to be more independent,[64] Faiza said to her mum last Friday that she "needs a carer now." It is as though she woke up determined to walk on Thursday, and on failing, realised how reliant she was on others. This is obviously not very nice for us, but I think it indicates an improvement in Faiza's level of awareness. Her dad asked her today when she thought she would get better (going against our rules for how to behave around Faiza), and she said she would be better in a week.

At Faiza's highest level of awareness, she is able to interact with us in a kind of conversation. For example, on Sunday morning I asked her what she thought of the meal I was about to feed her, and she said "it smells very nice." Later on I put some of Faiza's favourite music on. She said something that I couldn't quite understand first time, and when I asked her what it was she said she was "just singing along."

Faiza does, however, seem to spend much of the day day-dreaming. She prefers to do this in silence, but I have managed a few times to coax her into speech about it and to stimulate her gently from within the premises of her dream[65].

Early last week, Faiza frequently said the word "obscure": "things are obscure", "I'm obscure", and so on. I think now that this word certainly refers to the state of Faiza's consciousness (or rather, how she perceives things to be); at the start of last week, she was saying the word perhaps 50 times a day. An interesting example was when a new, trainee physio came into the room along with Rachel but didn't introduce herself to us: Faiza pointed at her and said "obscure". Saying this, Faiza has been using the word much less, which I think is a good thing as it indicates that she has more than just one word for expressing her perception of the world.

vii) <u>Tiredness</u>. Faiza has been very tired for the last two days, and slept for most of today (Tuesday). Owing to this tiredness, Faiza has said very little over the last few days – certainly much less than she is capable of saying. The easiest way for her to communicate her desires is still to nod 'yes' or 'no' to things.

---

[64] Ben now confesses to me that there was something he deliberately omitted from an email to my doctors: in fact I fell when he was helping me to stand up, even though I was clearly unable to. He did this because it was the only way to show me why I was heavily discouraged from getting up out of my wheelchair so often.

[65] Ben would talk to me in my daydreams to try to stimulate thought in my head. The conversation he had with me about "Khadija's sister" is probably the most psychologically significant.

viii) <u>Emotional wellbeing</u>. In line with Faiza's increasing awareness of her situation, she has been feeling rather low for the last two days.

Yesterday (Monday), I asked Faiza if she was OK. She shook her head, and then said a sentence to me that ended in the words "not lying", but I didn't quite hear the start of it and she wouldn't repeat it to me. My suspicion is that someone - perhaps the OT who had just seen Faiza - said something innocuous and well-intentioned like "go on, you can do that. You're lying to me", and Faiza took it to heart. I think this episode is useful because it shows i) Faiza's ability to converse, and ii) her ability to relate emotionally to her environment.

Faiza has since seemed to be very put out by her environment, and seems very agitated most of the time. I think this is probably a reasonable response to it, as i) she cannot be very comfortable physically, what with being unable to walk, and so on; ii) it is a lot of effort for Faiza to speak, and lots of people have been trying to force Faiza to say things for the sake of it; iii) Faiza has no real privacy, and her room can be invaded at any point by nursing staff, cleaners, etc., who can often be intrusively noisy at a time when Faiza is particularly sensitive to these things.

ix) <u>Background information</u>. You may not be aware of the following things about Faiza, which according to my understanding are factors in the outcomes of people with head injuries (although as you can tell, I am not a medic). Faiza was extremely intelligent before her accident, and studied Physics & Astrophysics at Cambridge, getting a 2.1. Also Faiza is an extremely strong-willed person; this is perhaps harder to quantify, but anybody who knows her would attest to it. At 26, I understand her to be at the ideal age for such a devastating injury to be sustained.

Take care everyone, and I hope to see you all soon.

Ben

Date: 1 April 2009 10:22
Subject: Update on Faiza
From: Benjamin Smith

Hello again all,

As last week, this is an edited version of the email I sent out to Faiza's doctors, so it might read a little strangely! I've pretty much just pasted it as a kind of appendix to this email.

Overall, we have seen a marked improvement in Faiza's condition over the week. Her GCS is still 14 - though a high 14 - but Faiza is much more alert and mobile. I think Faiza probably made bigger steps last week than we had realised. The changes were taking place behind the scenes, but we couldn't see them because, owing to her low mood, she spoke so little.

This is probably the first time since Faiza's accident that I have actually felt that my hopefulness has any ground in objective reality. Although saying that, all of the usual, horrible caveats still apply: with all head injuries, it appears that the outcome always very uncertain. I found have very helpful a maxim from an old Marxist philosopher[66] (!): we need to have optimism of the will, but pessimism of the intellect.

Faiza has also been asking to have lots of visitors! Now that she's so much more talkative, she likes to see people and hates being on her own. Weekends will, I'm hoping, still be busy, but if any of you do feel like coming then don't hesitate to at all. Faiza has been awake for most of the day, so she'd probably be awake when you're here (the only thing that might restrict time with her would be the limit on the number of visitors allowed in with her at one time).

Take care everyone, and see you soon.

Ben

xii) <u>Talking</u>

Just as she has been much more awake since last Friday, so Faiza has also been much more talkative. And not just delirious talk as before, but proper

---

[66] Ben often plays up to a reputation he has about his obsession with Marxism – his love of Marxist philosophy became something of a joke amongst our friends.

conversation. Faiza interacts with us all, and brings her own mind into the conversation. I would say that at the moment, talking to Faiza is like talking to a child of upper primary school age.

Faiza told me today that she is keen to spend as much time around people as possible, because when she's on her own she "thinks too much". She likes to keep busy, and has been asking me about when she can get back to her job. When I told her that she couldn't do that for the moment, she asked me if she could perhaps do some voluntary work in the hospital! This seems to show quite a high level of awareness of her environment, and of the sorts of possibilities that might (or in this case, might not) be available to her.

xiv) <u>Mood</u>

Faiza's mood has gotten better over the last week. On Friday, for example, she was feeling happy and said to a friend who had come to visit her that she didn't want any music on because she wanted to appreciate her friend while she was there. [67] Faiza also seemed happier on Friday because she had stood up in physio, and could therefore see some improvement in her physical condition.

However, Faiza's state when I arrived on Saturday morning is best described by the word 'terror'. She recognised who I was, but asked repeatedly where she was and what had happened to her. She was manic with fear, and it took the whole day to calm her down. She did calm down, though, when some friends came to visit. I think that friends are good for her at the moment because they provide a good balance of intimate friendliness and the distance that is needed to help her out of her doldrums.

xv) <u>Awareness</u>

Predictably, Faiza has been more aware of her situation and of the world around her. On Saturday, she could not take in the fact that she was in hospital, but by Monday she was consistently aware of this. She is also now consistently aware of the fact that she's in Oxford, and that she has been in a car accident. Faiza has problems remembering the date; I would say that just over 50% of the times that I have asked her, she knows that it's March 2009. At her best, she knows that it's near the end of March: my birthday was on the 26th, and she sometimes says that the date is after this, on the 27th. I think that most of the issues that last week

---

[67] My brain still tends to become overloaded by sensory input. Then, it struggled to concentrate even with background music on.

would have come under the heading of 'awareness' come under the heading of 'memory' this week.

A consequence of her improving awareness is that Faiza has been more cooperative about enduring discomfort/pain in her physio & in wearing the splints to keep her joints straight, as she is now more able to think about the long-term benefits of the immediate sacrifice of comfort.

xvi) <u>Memory</u>

Many of Faiza's long-term memories appear to be intact, and we have seen an improvement in this area over the last 4-5 days. She is now aware of the various places that we have lived over the last 7-8 years[68], and remembers all of her friends and relatives. Also, Faiza was telling me today about some obscure bits of physics that I don't know anything about! Her memory was a bit vague, but still there (for instance, she was talking about a 'Schwarzkopf's Law' of resistance, but I don't think she remembered it quite right).

Faiza is experiencing difficulty making new memories. For example, she didn't remember on Monday who had visited her on Sunday. This morning, though, she did "vaguely" remember that my grandparents had visited her the day before, so this may be improving (or alternatively it might just be that I asked her in the morning and not the afternoon).

Faiza can form some new memories though. For instance, when I arrive in the morning she can tell me reliably what has been happening that morning. Or, when she repeatedly called her nurse 'Nicola' instead of 'Karen' (Nicola is the name of a friend of ours, and I think that Karen reminded Faiza of Nicola), Faiza was eventually able to correct herself and call her Karen.

xvii) <u>Activities</u>

Faiza has been listening to some of her favourite music, and sometimes sings along to it, remembering all the words correctly.

---

[68] We had moved house several times - in the nine years preceding the date of that email, I had lived in a total of 12 different addresses. I'm not sure if Ben tested my knowledge of all of them!

8 Released

When I returned home from the OCE, it was late summer and the fields were rich with lush, green grass. The summer before, when we had just moved into our idyllic country escape, Ben and I went on a trip to the fields to pick blackberries. We hoped that jam-making would become something of an annual event. And this year there was nothing stopping this: I had been released, could walk and had all the time in the world. But my alienatation from the life I was living was so profound that I didn't do much more than run through the motions of living. I was just existing: I did not notice the summer beauty that we lived in.

Once I was released, I was seen by the 'crap OTs'... Or rather, I should say: after my discharge from the rehabilitation centre, my care was overseen by Oxfordshire county council's primary care trust (PCT). One of my activities to 'kill the days' was seeing healthcare professionals. Because I could not get to them, both the physiotherapist and Occupational Therapists would visit me at home[69].

I got on really well with the physio, Jenny. We would do stretches or sometimes go on a walk to the local church. When I was an inpatient at the OCE, I was given an A4 page of exercises that I could do unsupervised in my bedroom. They used to call this 'room gym' and I was told that I could carry these on when I was back at home. So I did.

Visits from the OTs, on the other hand, did not go so well: they insisted on helping me with my 'functioning', when I could not see what was wrong with it. I probably would not have said that I was 'back to the old me': I accepted that I had problems with my balance and memory, but that was the extent of it, wasn't it?

---

[69] Various cognitive effects of my head injury meant that I could not get myself to a healthcare worker. I had problems with my memory and changes to my visual processing. These were both most profound when I was on the spot. To put it crudely, this meant that if I did leave the house I would be unable to get myself to my destination and I would not remember my way back. (Both my map reading abilities and my sense of direction were of an unusually low standard.)

Ben now tells me how he thinks that the OTs had a very poor understanding of head injuries. Looking back, I can appreciate that with no specific training, they must have found it quite hard to appreciate why I had the impairments I did: there was nothing visibly wrong with me, yet I seemed to be unable to do the simplest of tasks. And to make it worse, I was difficult to talk to and could not see what the problem was.

In *The Man Who Mistook His Wife For A Hat,* Oliver Sacks comments explicitly on his patients' intelligence and sensitivity, alongside his discussions of their neurological impairments. Sacks may have seen how the force of an onlooker's intuitive perception of a patient's impairments can lead them to overlook the unexpected intelligence that patients can still possess. Sacks writes things such as, "She was intelligent and cultivated, fond of the ballet, and of the Lakeland poets." Nothing remarkable about that – until you understand that he is talking about a woman who is unable to make any sense of the sensory information from her own body. He is making the point that we should see the person, not just the condition.

So, when someone upset me, it was because THEY were annoying. Or if I was feeling generous then I knew that I should not blame them, because it was them who lacked interpersonal skills. They were just a bit thick, socially speaking. These incidents could also be explained by the fact that the person who had annoyed me knew that I had a head injury and was, therefore, prejudiced towards people like me. I told myself that this was understandable, because I had seen how bad some (other) head injured people could be.

The prejudice could also be explained by the fact that they had noticed my minor dysarthria. Dysarthria is how neurological damage causes speech to be poorly articulated and quieter. This was one of the things that Ben often cites as an example of how my functioning was affected. I don't think it was, but it must have been. Otherwise why would he lie? Why could I not tell? Was it because the acoustics in the skull make the voice sound different to the person speaking? Or is he just fussy? I guess I've just learnt to accept that there's no functional purpose in trying to answer these questions. But, the old Faiza's ravenous intellect would never have put up with that sort of fudging.

When these OTs observed, for example, that my affected spatial intelligence had rendered my map reading worse than useless, they extrapolated this low level across all my intellectual capacities. As a result they came to the conclusion that my head injury had made me globally dim. Given that they saw me only for three months, it must have been infuriating for them that my 'recovery' was virtually nonexistent. My functioning must have seemed profoundly affected, yet I acted like there was nothing wrong with me. Why was she being so difficult? Will she ever recover?

If they were familiar with head injuries, they would not use that word 'recovery'. The brain cells that died as my brain shook inside my skull as the car came to a halt will never come back. All that has happened since the crash is that the living neurones branch out and make new pathways. (This happens in all brains: damaged and healthy ones.) This is how head injury victims regain functioning, and is why the term 'enablement' is frequently favoured in neurological medicine.

***

Wednesday 16th September 2009

These two women came by today from the council. They're here to "reintegrate me back into society". I didn't realise I was out of society, but it looks like 'them upstairs' have decided that I am. I can't simply be released from hospital and just be allowed to live at home. No, that would be too simple. They have too much money to spend on this sort of stuff and I guess they have to spend it somehow.

They were OTs from the council. They just had to fill in a few forms. They asked me questions like "Do you wash and dress yourself independently?" So it was all quite bog standard stuff, really.

Then they asked "Do you cook?", and I explained how Ben's a bit of a kitchen Nazi and he had to intervene. [70] *I didn't want it to look like I'm under the thumb, so I added my own explanatory note: "He's always been like that".*

I don't see why the tiniest hint of any minor 'inequality' in a marriage is suddenly such a big deal now, especially because I think we're quite good in that department. But the tiniest indication that there might be an atom of inequality is now unacceptable, just because I'm disabled.

I also had the perennial problem that all these people have: trouble seeing irony if it slapped them in the face and danced a little jig. But I guess being blind to irony is their own visual impairment. Rather than be annoyed with their failure to spot it, we should

---

[70] Ben "intervened" because he had become attuned to the tendency that some medical professionals had to be a little judgemental over relatives' tendency to 'take over' and not let patients have their autonomy. He did not want to be tarred with this brush.

refrain from judging them for being so stupid. We could all spend a little time thinking about "how they're being so brave wrestling with all their difficulties".[71]

Then we had to make... yes, you guessed it... some targets. Anyway, it helped pass the time.

***

Now obviously, I do not think that the funds devoted to rehabilitating head injury survivors are excessive. I believe that we should increase funds for training non-specialist occupational therapists to better meet the needs of not just head-injured patients, but the vast majority of neurological conditions.

Charitable donations to Headway are just not as marketable as ones for Cancer Research, and government spending on OT training for treatment of neurological conditions might not be as popular as more frequent bin collections. But funding for widening access to specialist care for neurological conditions is important to help maintain the fair and equal society that we believe we live in.

***

Tuesday 22nd September 2009

Val [the OT assistant] came by today, unaccompanied by her boss. Our activity today was to plan our next session! This is why it takes so long after a head injury. Because they waste time filling out forms in triplicate and having faffy "activities".

I told her about the mosaic classes that I'm going to do for Headway and that I needed to learn the bus route to their daycentre for that. So we looked up the bus route and printed off a map for that.

Later she said, "Do you want to practice teaching the classes to me and Lyn?" I told her I didn't think that would be necessary, especially since I used to teach physics to really

---

71 My sarcastic tone was so exaggerated because I frequently encountered problems with successful communication of irony. When I was in the JR, often people would not realise that I was being sarcastic. Ben tells me how he made a sign for me, which read "JOKING" written in BIG BLACK CAPS and I was supposed to hold it up when I was being sarcastic. He tells me that he did this because people frequently would not realise that I was joking because, like many head injury survivors, I had difficulty expressing an appropriate tone in my voice. Also, the doctors and nurses to whom I would crack these jokes were busy at work and in a professional role. They were not in a position to spend time constructing their own witty remarks back. For me, it was always because they did not get the joke. (What other reason could there not be for not laughing at my hilarious observations?)

rough secondary school kids. [72] I then added that I'm doing this voluntary work to help me learn my impairments for when I want to return to my job as a teacher, and I pointed out how preposterous it was saying that I should build up to even that. I think it kind of takes the piss forcing me to take baby steps to learn how to walk just because I have difficulties running. Then I said to her "What will you suggest I do next: practice the class on midgets?"

So, they're going to come next week. Not to have a mosaic lesson. Just to go shopping.

Friday 25th September 2009

Val came by and we went on a trip into Oxford (just to buy some shampoo). Why Ben couldn't just pop out in his lunch hour I don't know: I guess they want to make me 'independent'. You can't just go asking your husband to pop into Boots in your lunch hour. He's a working man! That's what his taxes go on: making sure that cripples like me aren't too dependent (leaching off members of our taxpaying public).

She was quite annoying the whole way. Always giving me helpful advice about how I should do things safely. Like, make sure I look both ways before crossing the road. This was before I'd even stepped up to the crossing! What was I thinking, not voicing my intention to follow the 'green cross code' ten seconds before reaching the curb?! Clearly I have to be more cautious now that I'm disabled. She fails to appreciate that she doesn't have to make me think like the risk-averse middle aged old biddy that she wants me to be, now that I'm crippled. [73]

---

[72]The "really rough secondary school kids" that I taught were at my previous school in Camden. A significant proportion of children were entitled to free school meals, which is a statistic often used as an indicator of the children's social background. This is a fact I often remind myself of, when I feel that I would not be able to cope outside the comfort of my cushioned, middle-class life.

[73] I needed to act in a way that I considered to be "risk averse" because a brain injury can affect the victim's perception of risk. In fact, someone who has sustained a head injury is several times more likely to sustain a subsequent head injury after the initial one. It is difficult, however, to attribute this to a single factor. Often the victim's sense of balance, vision and/or perception of physical sensation, have been affected. Other cognitive impairments, aside from judgment of risk, can also increase the risk. (They might, for example, be disinhibited and get into a fight while out for a drink at the pub.)

Or they might have sustained the original injury because they involve themselves in risk-taking behaviour, which increased their chances of sustaining another head injury. In my case, maybe I crashed the car because I was driving too fast. The OTs, however, put my different perception of risk down to neurological damage from the head injury, but perhaps it was this alternative perception of risk, which made me sustain the head injury in the first

When we were walking home from the bus stop, she told me off for cutting across the green. She said that it's not safe because it's not level ground, and I should go along the smooth tarmac that goes around it. I couldn't be bothered to argue so we took the long route.

Unfortunately she could see through my thin veil of polite nods and smiles and made me agree with her that she was right and that I should go round the outside. It was sort of like getting me to go via Shipton-on-Cherwell. [74] *So I "promised" that I wouldn't cut across the green if I was by myself.*

Then when we were home she did yet another annoying thing. I had to get something from upstairs and she 'advised me' to make sure I switch the light on before going up the stairs. This was in the middle of the day! I protested saying "I do have pupils in my eyes. I don't think they were damaged in the car crash!"

Sadly I've decided that things will have to change now. A polite: "Oh yes, thank you. I hadn't thought of the ridiculous risks that a cripple like me couldn't possibly afford to take". And then use my own judgement and continue 'to balance inches away from the cliff edge' in her dangerphobic middle aged mind...

***

The next few months passed by with more visits from these OTs. They visited me every week, sometimes twice a week. They continued to annoy me.

***

Thursday 1ˢᵗ October 2009

I talked to Ben about how these OTs are doing my nut in and I don't want to see them anymore. He pointed out how I have to give him credit for seeing it from my point of view, but he just couldn't appreciate the extent to which they're annoying.

---

place. Shortly after I had been discharged from hospital, when I had difficulty sleeping, this is the sort of thing that I might be thinking as I lay in bed awake at night.

[74] Around the outside of the green is less than 50% longer, but I did tire quite easily, so it felt like adding on a massive distance. I often joked about how going around the green was akin to going via Shipton-on-Cherwell, a neighbouring village about 3 miles away. (I would make this joke to show off the fact that I had remembered the name of this tiny village.)

But when I said I didn't think I needed them anymore, he was quite annoying about it all. He reckons that if I get rid of them then I'm throwing the baby out with the bath water. In my defence I did tell him that they're doing way more harm than good. [75]

It's true that they occupy my days and do MILDLY useful jobs. But that is at the cost of my self-esteem and, ironically, my independence. Ben said that I should say to them that I want to see them just once a fortnight from now on. He said he'll try and work from home on the days when I see them, to act as a bit of a buffer.

I'm not happy with that: it's not a solution. I don't want to waste one of my days when he's around by sharing him with a middle-aged Beelzebub.

So I've agreed to keep them on, but just seeing them less often, which is something. But they always act like I'm not recovering, when everyone else is always telling me "how well I'm doing".

Their annoyingness could also explain why they seem to act like I'm not trying hard enough to get better. According to their logic I should be fixed by now. They think that laziness is the only explanation of why there's still loads 'wrong' with me. [76]

But there's nothing really wrong with me anyway: I am 'better'! They just act like everything that's different about me is BECAUSE of this head injury. They don't seem to realise that it's just because I'm intelligent and have a different outlook on life from them.

Ben was saying that they do stuff like take me on the bus. So I explained to him that "you could do that with me just as well".

I can't remember exactly what he said [77]*, but it made me think that I can't just assume that being around me is fun for him. They do have "breaks for carers" at Headway. I can*

---

[75] I have since spoken to Ben about how the OTs did "more harm than good" and he has helped me appreciate what the difficulties of the situation were. I had an affected *theory of mind*: I had difficulty 'decentring' and taking a view that was alternative to my own. On top of this, my impaired social skills meant that I had no tolerance for the nonsense I thought the OTs were talking. All of these things combined to make OT a very un-therapeutic experience for me, and this, rather than the OTs necessarily being bad, was why Ben let me sack them.

[76] Often patients with head injuries are labelled as 'lazy' because of how the neurological damage presents itself. As well as affecting a person's functioning the injury can affect the survivor's ability to initiate tasks. Victims can also appear disorganised and have affected memory. As a result it can appear as though we could just try a bit harder.

[77] Ben says he cannot remember exactly what he said either. He might not have a damaged brain, but it has been two years.

understand that for carers of people who need to be washed and dressed. Even though I can do that myself, maybe there's still something else to this equation. Am I difficult to be around? I guess I'd better start pulling my own weight.

Ben says he's read on the 'net that a big part of restarting your life after head injury is about acceptance of what's wrong with you and not just expecting the body to fix itself by magic. Once the brain cells are dead, they're dead. There's no arguing with biology.

But Val acts as though, "I'm sure if you put in a bit of effort you could recover" and, "Well, they're not going to spring back to life if you have that kind of attitude, are they?".

I want him to stick up for me when they're here because even me, Miss 'Take No Shit from Anyone', can't stand up for herself now.

***

Eventually I managed to convince Ben that the OT I was getting was not working. But he would not agree with me when I said that I would be better off without any Occupational Therapy. What is more, everyone I spoke to took Ben's side and advised me to persevere with them and implied that I should stop being so difficult. They were probably motivated by thoughts that I was just another 'difficult head injury patient'. Perhaps I was. Or perhaps these patients all struggle to communicate with others who fail to appreciate the exact nature of the problems they face.

By the autumn of 2009, Ben let me free myself from the clutches of the crap OTs. At the time I thought that I would no longer need OTs to interfere with my life, watch my functioning and deem it to be insufficient to manage an independent life. But Ben worked hard to have me referred back to the OCE because he still thought that I was not 'fixed'.

"Why does everyone seem to be obsessed with telling me that I was so disabled? They can't even tell me what's wrong with me."

***

Scene: A lounge with a fireplace. The fire is lit and Faiza and Ben are seated next to each other on a light brown, three-seater sofa. The room is filled with various items: old newspapers, books, and discarded used crockery. There are also at least two guitars balancing precariously against an amp placed across the other side of the room by a matching two-seater settee.

Ben has on a T-shirt under a blue towelling dressing gown and Faiza is wearing some spotty pyjamas. Both are drinking mugs of tea.

FAIZA: Benny, can you steal me a notebook from your work when you get the chance?

BEN: Yeah, sure. If I remember.

FAIZA: Now I'm not working, I only have you for stationery.

BEN: [laughs] Yeah, that's all that work's good for.

FAIZA: [laughing] And photocopying. That's why I want to go back to work.

BEN: Hmm.

FAIZA: When do you think I can?

BEN: [with an irritated voice] I don't know.

FAIZA: OK, not this September, but the next one?

BEN: Look, Faiza… it's so hard to say.

FAIZA: But, why can't I go back?

BEN: We've talked about this.

FAIZA: But why?

BEN: It'll take more time before you're better.

FAIZA: But, what's wrong with me?

BEN: There's nothing WRONG with you.

FAIZA: Exactly.

BEN: But… it's just hard to describe.

FAIZA: Try.

BEN: I guess as a teacher you need to be able to speak to groups.

FAIZA: My dysarthria?

BEN: Yeah, sort of.

FAIZA: Is it so bad that people wouldn't be able to understand me? I think I'm perfectly intelligible. And if I do those exercises, I should be ready by June. What else? I guess my memory?

BEN: [hesitantly] Well, yeah.

FAIZA: But I can make adjustments. I've been thinking about it. I can expand my register into an exercise book, so I can write little notes to help me keep track of kids' progress. Or I could write in little comments like "struggled with exercise on momentum".

BEN: Yeah, I guess so.

FAIZA: Exactly.

BEN: I just think it'll do no harm to wait.

FAIZA: But I want to go back.

BEN: That's something I read on the Headway website: that it's quite a common mistake to rush back to study or employment.

FAIZA: But doesn't it also say how all head injuries are different, and you have to judge each case on its own.

BEN: [uneasily] Hmmm.

FAIZA: Can I at least try?

BEN: I just think that it's better to wait.

FAIZA: If I try and fail then you can get your way in the end.

BEN: OK, if you want you can email Summertown [college].

FAIZA: Really?

BEN: Yeah, OK.

FAIZA: And you'll support me?

BEN: Of course. Look, I just want what's best.

FAIZA: Yeah, I know you do. It's just that YOU think that waiting is what's best.

BEN: Look, I'm on your side.

FAIZA: I know. [With resignation] And you're really understanding.

BEN: Look, come here, you big silly.

FAIZA: I know I'd be stupid to complain... I have everything, don't I?

BEN: Look, it's OK... This is all hard.

FAIZA: And I've coped really well, haven't I?

BEN: [smiling] Yeah.

***

On a day when I was not seeing the 'crap OTs' I would be at home alone. Not being able to enjoy the same things that I used to drove me mad. Or rather, I wish that I could say that it drove me mad, but that overlooks the worst thing about this time: I did not even have the luxury of telling myself that this life was different to the one that I had before. My brain just could not compute that.

I couldn't leave the house, so I struggled to pass the time. I couldn't even watch TV. I wasn't really able to follow involved storylines, appreciate the subtle humour or fast wit in the TV programmes that the 'old Faiza' liked. And I always thought that mindless American sitcoms were too stupid for me – even my damaged brain would find them painfully predictable.

I couldn't take pleasure in reading either, as I was unable to make sense of what was written. (Audio books weren't much better.) One of the most penetrating effects of the head injury was a virtual inability to pick up on the finer qualities of life. For instance, I had double vision and my sense of smell and taste became much cruder.

I always felt that I had to justify my existence to the 'old Faiza': she would not look too kindly on someone who spends the days watching repeats of old American sitcoms. And it would kill me when I could not even follow them (I did not have the required memory or concentration).

There was very little I could do to occupy myself and enjoyment of the finer things in life was a laughable concept. I found it hard to explain this to people who were not familiar with the life of a head injury victim. 'Cognitive impairments' are the words used to describe what people with brain injuries suffer, which could stop them from functioning and living a 'normal' life. Often people reduce cognitive impairments to no more than memory problems. But memory problems were just the tip of the iceberg (and even memory problems are more involved than people might initially think).

I used to love painting. I would look at the fine details in a view (the shades of light and dark, the strong sweep of a line or the subtle textures on an object). But now I just looked: light entered my pupils.

So, because it was clear to any observer that I should not be left at home alone - but not to me because after all, I was better - Ben would take me to Ami [Mum] and Daddy's house. I left a toothbrush and some clothes there, so I could be taken in my pyjamas. I thought he would just drop me off on his way to work, but it was in fact a total detour of an hour and a half in London traffic after spending a day in the office, which was a break from caring for his disabled wife. Survivors and their carers often have to wrestle with the victim's lack of awareness and, although this was a very mild case, it was no exception.

I remembered having a difficult relationship with my parents, but nowadays I seemed to get on much better with them. "Perhaps it's because of my head injury," I thought, "I've heard about how they can cause a personality change".

It was not exactly the head injury, Ben tells me. He says that my relationship with my parents was already starting to improve as I got older. Reading between the lines of my old emails does confirm this to some extent, but don't we all just see what we look for? I remembered my parents as the people I blamed for my teenage depression, but now I could see how the situation was a bit more complex than that, and I seemed be working through it all.

So I would go to Harrow and enjoy spending the day with my parents. It definitely seemed that a lot had changed while I had been asleep in my coma! On other days Ben would sneak me into his office. (He works as a textbook writer at a college in Shepherd's Bush.) I would sit in the basement study area ready with the line "I'm just here on a course" if anyone ever asked who I was, but no one ever did. There

I could listen to my iPod to pass the time. As I became more able, I would use the college's student computers to play solitaire or browse the internet. Ben would pop down periodically during the day to "get the people in his office drinks from the basement's vending machine".

Eventually, I was able enough to be walked to the nearby shopping centre. We would have lunch there and then I would spend the afternoon doing some important window shopping until he came to collect me so that we could go home at 5.

These trips helped me deal with the fact that I could not be trusted at home alone all day, every day.

***

If this book is about my return to life, or re-entering it with my new brain, then as well as talking about how I would while away the days, I need to mention the whole benefits saga. [78] Sometime in the autumn of 2010 a lady from the council visited us, and she seemed very surprised, after seeing how undisabled I looked, that the DWP (Department of Work and Pensions) had deemed me as eligible for the higher rate on both the mobility and care component of the disabled persons living allowance (DLA). I told her that we were not benefits cheats; we just knew how to fill a form in. [79]

---

[78] We seemed to be in an eternal battle with either the insurance company or the Department of Work and Pensions or both. At the time I was not able to understand much of it and what I can understand now is that it is both very complicated and very boring ...

The insurance company would make deductions for the benefits that I should be receiving, but the DWP would claim at the same time that the insurance money I was receiving meant that I was not eligible. This was an ongoing battle which still has not been fully resolved.

[79] The benefits application form is difficult to fill in for all disabilities, but is especially difficult for someone affected cognitively from the head injury and who has a disability as a result of a neurological condition. Head injuries are often called 'the invisible disability' because survivors' functioning can be enormously affected, but often with no obvious, outward signs.

Like most disabled people on benefits I feel the need to justify being in receipt of them. The reason that Ben and I were deemed eligible for the higher rate of the care component was probably because his night's sleep would be disturbed. This was because he would have to get up in the night, a) to take off my splint, and b) to help me to the toilet, which was a frequent occurrence at night because I had much reduced control over my urinary sphincter muscles (as a result of the catheter that I had been fitted with in hospital, combined with neurological damage).

Also, having talked at length about my experience of the crap OTs, I think I should say something positive about the PCT: it wasn't all bad. Jenny (my physio) referred me to the local leisure centre. She did this through a scheme called 'exercise on prescription', by which patients could be referred to a local gym.

'Exercise on prescription' is used for people who needed to be encouraged to exercise for health reasons. Ben often takes delight in teasing me about how it is really meant for obese people. Regardless, what this meant was that I could go the leisure centre in Bicester on Monday or Wednesday mornings for just £3. The reduced cost was especially important to me because I had enormous guilt as a result of me not being able to "pay my 50%", as I put it. (My income had dropped substantially as a result of my head injury, added to which we had no idea what sort of income I would be able to provide, or would demand, in the long run.[80])

Nearly a whole year after my crash (and this was, I am told, a major achievement), I was able to go to the gym independently by bus. At first, however, I could not get myself there. Wednesdays were one of Ben's half days, so this is when he would drive me. I resented using up one of my precious afternoons with Ben to go to the gym. But as time went on, I became adept at finding ways to kill time without demanding too-high-a-level of cognitive functioning, so my resentment reduced.

There was a minor admin problem which meant I did not receive my disabled bus pass for a couple of months (which seemed like an eternity for someone who had profound difficulties being able to pass their days meaningfully). This is why I only went to the gym once a week. But when it did arrive, for two afternoons a week I would get the number 25 bus to Bicester and go to the leisure centre. This helped

---

And although the higher rate of the mobility component is often only given to wheelchair users, it was probably given to me because I was housebound. I was housebound because of the enormous risk of me forgetting my way home if I did ever 'escape' (or leave the house), which was exacerbated by the fact that we had only recently moved into the area, and I could not learn where I lived because I could not form new memories. I had also become more uptight and prone to stress since my head injury, which meant, especially early on, that I did not have the courage to leave the safety of my house by myself. (Or rather, I did not have the "initiative" to leave the house when everyone else told me I couldn't because I was, apparently, "disabled".) I think I should also state that Ben filled in the benefits forms. I simply liked to tell myself that "we" filled in the forms well.

[80] The reason we did not know what our financial situation would be in the long run was because Ben had read hundreds of horror stories on the internet about the insurance company refusing to acknowledge that a disability prevented a beneficiary from working in their old job. (Or rather, the company had an alternative view on whether the beneficiary was able to return to work.) I was caught in the typical Catch-22 that many disabled people find themselves in: we are ill-advised to earn money by working.

give my week some sort of a structure. Or as I put it at the time "it helped to distract me as I managed to get closer to the end".

9 Days

On February 13th 1972, 33 year-old French geologist, Michel Siffre, climbed into Midnight Cave near Del Rio, Texas. He didn't come out again until September 5th. So, for six months he was isolated in a large cave chamber 440-feet from the entrance. It was bare down there. His tent was a on a wooden platform and in it there was a bed, chair, table and various machines for some science experiments.

He lived in total isolation in this underground cave and didn't have a clock. He was underground, so he couldn't even see the Sun. He only slept and ate when his body told him to. Since there was no one to talk to, his days melded into one bald expanse. He had no memorable events to act as landmarks as he went along the passageway of time. He did this to discover how the natural rhythms of human life would be affected by living in a land that he called "beyond time."

When the support team on the surface finally called down to him on, his journal said that it was only August 20th: his experience of time's passage had been massively compressed. Monotony collapses time. Memories unfold it.

I could not form memories, so like Siffre, my time had collapsed into one featureless blob.

Towards the end of the OCE the OTs had been telling me that people like me have difficulties with time. I have now come to accept that I probably did have some kind of "impairment": my ability to judge time was poor. The appropriate amount of time it would take me to cook a recipe was always way off the mark, because I foolishly thought that I could use the amount of time suggested on the website. I did not realise that I should double it because they would stipulate that I use a long-winded, laborious method they deemed necessary for someone like me.

Now these crap OTs were suggesting that I wear a watch all the time, because they had presumably heard that head injury survivors can have difficulty understanding the concept of time. (This can be anything from reading a clock correctly, judging what a minute, day, week, month or year feels like, or simply estimating an appropriate length of time to complete a given task.)

I knew that, factually, time had moved forward. Perhaps we were at a new place on the calendar or, if I was taken outside and it was pointed out to me, I could see that that the flowers had bud or that leaves had fallen off the trees. But it all felt the same.

"We all get that", people would reassure me. But today I can't even remember how long it has been since the new me was born.

***

Because of the retrograde amnesia that I suffered, I had "lost" about two years. Nothing especially dramatic had happened in that time, but I had completed a degree, moved house and started a new job. This all took a bit of adjusting to.

Everyone always talks about how "the world is moving so fast", and to me it seemed that this had happened overnight. When I was in my coma, Ben had bought a new mobile phone. I would not believe him when he reassured me that he hadn't blown all our cash on this elaborate piece of machinery and that this is just "what they are like now".

There were new programmes on TV. I did not recognise any of the songs on the radio. No-one bought newspapers, they downloaded them off the internet.

I found this all quite strange, something I mentioned in a diary entry:

Friday 18th September 2009

...Had an appointment at the hospital today. Ben was at work, so I had to get a taxi. I'm like an old lady now and think "back in the day £25 for a 5 minute tax ride was unthinkable... when I was a youngster it used to cost ha'penny". There must have been some kind of hyper-inflation when I was in a coma, like they had in post-WWI Germany...

***

Tuesday 12th October 2010

The OTs came round again and we talked about stuff or "activities" we could do to help with my reintegration. And meet my all-important targets.

I love the way that they're "our" targets. I don't want my name associated with their pointless little world of activities. Especially not such stupid, measurable tick boxes: "achievements" that I'm suddenly supposed to find really meaningful and worthwhile.

Why can't they just be honest with me and say "We know they're pointless, but we've got to pretend that they're really big to sustain the illusion that your life is meaningful. We want to keep you occupied, while we stop you getting ahead of yourself with some little deluded idea about going back to work."?

They helpfully suggested that to help with my time management I wear a watch ALL the time. They asked, "If you don't wear a watch how do you manage your time?" I didn't yell in their faces "I don't want to 'manage my time', I just want to live my life". Instead, I explained it to them like a normal person, and told them that this is my time off sick and I don't want to ruin it by having my life governed by time.

I told them how [as a teacher] I bought a digital watch specifically for the purpose of showing the kids who's boss. [81] "I'm off sick from work. My life doesn't have to be governed by a watch now. Please don't ruin this time for me." They exchanged looks that translated into "Well, she obviously doesn't want to get better".

I then went on my rant about how society invented a special instrument to tell the time, specifically to strap to our arms. Somewhat hilariously, they then enquired about my "time and clocks are everywhere" hypothesis and looked round the room for some empirical evidence to support this – all they could see was that funky, swirly one from Kilburn High Road, with no numbers on its face.

What I have a problem with is that this head injury seems to affect EVERYTHING. Various people in various places seem to act like all of me has been affected by this head injury. Especially these fucking OTs. They seem to think my entire "functioning" has been affected.

Ben's crap with time, but no one tells him off. It's so unfair that he's allowed to get away with it, but in me it's apparently part of my disability that I need to take steps to overcome.

***

---

[81] As a teacher, I had learnt that it was to my advantage to give students the impression that I took pleasure in doing things such as closing the register at precisely 8:45 (after setting my watch to the second by the BBC news), and marking anyone who arrived after that as late and then following up with my petty detention rules.

None of these professionals ever asked me what I felt about time. And even if they did, I wouldn't have been able to understand what was being talked about, let alone explain it.

But for me, the days never felt like days. They were nothing more than an arbitrary unit that the able-brained population decided that periods should be divided into.

Now I no longer had days, what could life mean?

10 Kew Gardens

I remember a few of us sitting in the classroom one lunch time. We were in 'lower fifth', or year nine to people who went to a normal school. My parents chose to save up their hard earned money and send me to a ridiculously posh private school, because the children did much better there and I would "get admission to doctory[82]". The fact that all children had to be sufficiently hard working and intelligent in order to pass an 11+ entrance exam (and come from families who valued education enough to spend thousands of pounds a year on it), was always conveniently overlooked by most evaluations of the school.

Anyway, everyone in the classroom was chatting about what we'd do to celebrate Elizabeth's birthday. I say *we* were all chatting, but I was busy looking at my shoes, mentally preparing myself for people's looks of pity. It was well understood that I would not be going, because everyone knew how my parents would never allow me to go to a sleepover and spend the night away from family supervision. Since we had been at this school for over two years, all the girls knew what the deal was.

Then the bell rang for physics and we all got our books together. It was one of the only subjects I was any good at. The reason for this was that Naveed was excellent at physics and would teach me to a ludicrously high level, just through everyday chit-chat. I remember when I was ten, him explaining to me which of the biscuits that we were eating, was the strongest. (Incidentally it was the Garibaldi, because its structure replicates that of a composite material. The raisins can absorb the load while the floury dough simply transmits it, holding the main structure together, giving the overall biscuit a high strength to mass ratio.)

---

[82] It was common for second generation British South Asians at that time to feel that there was cultural pressure to study medicine. "Getting admission to study doctory" was something that my parents and their friends often talked about. Their use of Indian-English somehow symbolised to me their unfamiliarity with the career options open to British children my age.

We were getting results back from a test that we had done the previous lesson. Meera Shah, one of the cleverest girls in the class, would always start crying as the marked papers were handed back. This periodic event was something of a class joke because there would be tears rolling down her cheeks when she had scored a "pathetic" result that was a good 20% higher than any of our own scores. Looking back I can see that this was symptomatic of an overachieving school where eating disorders, amongst other adolescent mental health disorders, were by no means uncommon.

On Mondays I would be allowed to stay late because I went to Drama club. I had no massive love for performance, but like all adolescents, I wanted to go only because my friends did. I was always discouraged from going, because it would mean getting 'the late coach' home. The standard school coaches would depart straight after school, at 4:15, but the late coach would leave at 5:30, taking an especially long route. I did see Ami's point of view that its arrival time of 6:45 did seem quite late for a 13 year-old child to arrive home after school, but I still fought the battles to have this one little freedom. I never minded getting home late from school: in many ways I felt more alive there.

Later that week I had Biology. This year we had already started on the GCSE syllabus, because two years was not enough for the excessive detail in which the school wanted to teach the syllabus. So they had to start teaching the GCSE a year early, in year 9. A decade later, when I taught the circulatory system, I would get my students to enact a model of the blood system, with each pupil playing the role of a red-blood cell carrying 'oxygen' (red pieces of card) to an area of the laboratory where a child we called 'the rest of the body' would take them. Instead, at my school I was labelling a black and white diagram with names such as the 'superior vena cava'.

Mrs Goldberg told us to make sure that we teamed up so that there was "at least one bloodthirsty girl in each pair". Katherine was a vegetarian and could not understand how cutting up an actual organ that had pumped inside a living being was necessary for educational purposes. Mrs Goldberg definitely would have branded her 'squeamish'. Seeing as I was looking forward to a double lesson devoted to butchery, it was decided that we would be an ideal match. "More blood for me."

After lunch that day we had geography. My year group had recently been on a trip to Kew Gardens and we were all composing articles about it to go in the school magazine. We were allowed to work in pairs on this, so Naraayanie and I worked together. My parents had recently bought me and Naveed a computer for schoolwork. So I was going to take home what Naraayanie and I wrote in class, then type it up before handing it in.

In bed that night, I lay awake thinking "the pills are just waiting for you downstairs. The longer you leave this the more pills will get used up". Whether I genuinely wanted to 'take the plunge' was not something I ever really questioned. I just knew that it was something I had to do.

"Why?" you may ask. "Too much pressure to do well at school." "Expectation that I would have an arranged marriage." These were the reasons that various people proposed after my admission to hospital, but they never really hit the nail on the head.

I just had a feeling that I did not deserve life and was a drain on people. I would only grow up to be a disappointment to them. It was better if I acted now, while I still had promise, rather than take the plunge and break their hearts after failing to deliver. These thoughts are not a million miles away from the ones I would later have after my car crash.

My idea that I was a drain on my family parallels the idea I had later that I was a drain on the able-bodied world. I had always taken solace in the idea that I was an able net contributor to society, and never learnt to handle being a "taker". I had to break down my childish ideas about "givers" and "takers" and submit to the concept that this is the life that God has chosen for all of us: both givers and takers. After my head injury I had to confront these same feelings all over again, and this time I would have to do it head on.

***

On Thursday, we had the day off school because the school needed to be vacated, as the prospective first year students were sitting the 11+ entrance exam. So I met up with my closest friend, Naraayanie. The plan was that her dad would drop her round to my house in the morning and then pick her up after work.

Before she arrived I put on the blue mascara that I had bought while out shopping with her, because she said it "looks really funky". I did not spend too long getting ready, because I knew this would only count against me. Blue jeans and a checked shirt gave the right impression that I was not too bothered about how I looked.

When she came by in the morning, we chatted and listened to music. Nirvana was one of our favourite bands and Naraayanie had brought round her cassette of *Bleach*, so that I could copy it. After that, the plan was to go to *Video Viking* on

Kenton Road and rent a video. We were definitely going to try and rent out something that was at least a 15. So, we went up to my parents' bedroom and 'borrowed' some of Ami's lipstick. We chose the most garish colours that we could, trying not to look like two school girls, indulging in an activity that the British Board of Film Classification deemed as unsuitable for their innocent little minds.

We successfully rented out the latest Quentin Tarantino bloodbath, *Pulp Fiction*, and brought it back to the house to watch. I watched it again years later, once I was over the required age of 18. If I am honest, I can see that most of it had gone over my head, perhaps because the second time I was not anxiously focussed on appearing as though I was just lying back and enjoying the film.

Then we looked at Teletext to see when the new Brad Pitt film, *Seven*, would be showing in the local Harrow cinema. I knew that all girls fancied him, so even though I had no burning feelings for him, I said that I wanted to see Seven because I thought "Brad Pitt's fit".

Afterwards, we caught a bus to Harrow-on-the-Hill, and 'went shopping' before the film started. What going shopping meant for two girls with no income of their own, was browsing in shops expressing what they thought was cool about various items. In my case (perhaps for Naraayanie too – but I doubt it), this meant looking at clothes and records and expressing a liking for the sorts of things that I had heard other girls said "had attitude".

We got the bus back to my house and then Naraayanie's dad came to collect her. After she left Naveed, Ami and I settled down to dinner. Daddy was away working managing air conditioning systems for an oil firm in Saudi Arabia. He had been away for several months now and it would be three more before he would be back. As we ate our karhai chicken and rice, the phone rang because someone wanted to come and see a room in Clauson Avenue. (My family owned a house in Sudbury, and rented out the rooms for additional income. [83])

So that evening Ami and Naveed left me home alone. I felt quite alone and desperate, like most days. To comfort myself I took a vegetable knife out of the kitchen drawer and used it to cut myself. Normally, I would cut myself on my arms (from my wrist to my elbow) and today was no exception. But I had never used

---

[83] My family managed the house directly because they did not believe in letting it through an agent. They much preferred to put in some hard graft and save the 10% they would have otherwise had to pay – this, I like to think, is the work ethic that is hard-wired into my brain that helped me fight back from death's door.

the kitchen knife before. I remember having to stop to answer the phone because the prospective tenant was lost and needed further directions. This was in the days before mobile phones, so I had to give them myself. Then I began to cut again.

I cannot really say why I did it. I have read since then that the feeling of pain releases endorphins in the sufferer's brain and gives a relief to the numbness of depression. This is said to be akin to an emotional high. I thought that I would cut myself to help relieve frustration and at the time I used to tell myself it was a form of punishment for failing to live up to expectations. What specifically these expectations were, I never really articulated; there was just some general sense that I was a huge disappointment. After all, what did I have to be unhappy about?

Then, after a few moments, I cannot really say how long, I threw the knife across the kitchen and screamed. I let it land on the tiled floor with a clatter. I remember berating myself for thinking that inflicting pain on myself would in some way bring a solution to the sense that something in me had 'gone wrong'. I thought to myself "They'll be back soon. Now's your chance".

I went and opened the kitchen cupboard and took out the paracetamol. I took them out in my hand and counted twenty-two. I knew this would never be enough, but I had to start somewhere. I put them in my mouth anyway and took a little sip of water being careful not to swallow too much because, as I had learnt whilst watching ER, it has a diluting effect on the chemicals in your stomach.

Postponing this any longer would only mean that more pills would be used up and make any possible future attempts yet more pathetic. I could wait until Ami replenished the supply, but I had no idea how long that would be.

I think I knew that so few pills would never be enough to do the job. I don't really know why I took them. Perhaps it was a form of self-harm. Through reading articles about the practice I have learned that swallowing several tablets can cause a physical reaction, which can act as an expression of the emotional pain that is felt. I knew that most successful attempts were always preceded by at least one failure, so if I was serious about it then I had better get started soon. Or maybe it was just a "cry for help".

I've always hated that expression; it never really explained much to me. Reasons for suicide can vary, and it can be a mixture of different things that finally leads someone to take their own life. It could be a desire to escape an existence that is felt too painful to bear, with death coming as a release. Or perhaps the choice of death might be seen as some sort of service to the people left behind. Looking back, I guess mine probably included both these 'reasons'. It probably was "a cry for help", since by choosing death I tried to express the fullness of the life I wanted myself and others to lead, instead of the mere survival that had been laid out for me. Choosing death seemed to articulate more about me than my actual life ever could.

If I wanted the paracetamol to work, I knew I would have to supplement them with something else and hope for a reaction. So, I went upstairs to the medicine drawer in my parents' room. The 'hardest drug' that I could see in there was a pack of Imodium (left over to treat the inevitable diarrhoea that we would fall victim to on trips to Pakistan). I took some of these. All that remained in the drawer, to my disappointment, was of no use to me (antiseptic cream, plasters and such like). I went downstairs to the fridge and all I could see was a bottle of Benylin. In desperation, I held the bottle to my lips and took a swig. The taste was horrible at the best of times, but this time, I did not allow myself a glass of water because of the effect water would have on the tablet concentration in my stomach.

I knew that Ami and Naveed would be back shortly, so I put the empty bottle of paracetamol back in the cupboard, replacing the screw top. I went upstairs and hastily shut the medicine drawer and began to work before they suspected that anything had gone awry. I had to work on the school magazine article about Kew Gardens that Naraayanie and I had written. It was my job to type it up and hand it in, so I thought I'd better get down to it.

My head was swimming as I worked. I was glad to see that the pills were having some effect, but I blocked out the sensations, focussing on the typing. Then, I was about to vomit, so I ran to the bathroom. Shortly after I had vomited in the sink, Ami discovered me.

After some time she came in and did what any Pakistani mother would do at a moment like this – enquired after my bowel movements. "*Dust bee array hai?*" [Are you getting diarrhoea too?] As she began musing out loud what could have caused this food poisoning, she headed off to her medicine drawer to fetch some Imodium for the diarrhoea she was expecting.

I was frightened that she would see that someone had been manically rummaging through the useless plasters and bandages, and I knew that there was no hope that the paracetamol had worked, so I decided to come clean. I spoke to her in English, something she would always tell me off for. "There's something you should know: I've taken an OD". She, almost certainly, had no idea that OD stood for overdose.

She probably thought that it was teen slang for some sort of illegal drug, like 'E', that I had picked up from my immoral school friends.

"*Patanay kya bolree hai*" [I don't know what she's saying], "Naveed!" He came upstairs and took over.

"Right, we'll have to take you to hospital," he said.

We all got into the Datsun Sunny and he drove us to Northwick Park Hospital A&E. Upon arriving, Naveed walked like a man in familiar territory. He was a third year medical student at the time, so he probably knew these sorts of environments. All I knew about Casualty was the long queues for which it was notorious. Naveed walked straight up to a lady in a brown jumper, who must have been a receptionist, and stated, quite unapologetically, "My sister's taken an overdose".

I was taken straight to a bay and asked a series of questions by a young white man. I'm guessing that he must have been a junior doctor. I felt sick and vomited into a sink that was beside the bed. The doctor then leant across the bay and retrieved a small cardboard dish, which he handed to me, stating "I don't think you're meant to be sick into those". "Oh, I'm so sorry. I didn't realise," I said, feeling guilty for the poor sap lumbered with the job of unblocking it and cleaning up somebody else's vomit.

I presumed that I would be in school tomorrow − it was not very likely that 22 paracetamol tablets would do the job, especially in light of my recent vomiting.

 "Tell me, what did you take?"

"Paracetamol."

"And did you have anything to drink?"

"I had some water."

"I meant anything alcoholic," he said, rubbing my nose in how clueless I was.

"No."

"We're Muslim. We don't drink alcohol," Ami triumphantly announced.

"Just as well," he stated. "How many paracetamol do you think you had?"

"Oooh - I don't know, whatever was in the bottle."

"How many is that?"

"I don't know. A few." I was not going to cooperate.

But Ami, like any good Pakistani woman running a well-oiled household, could recall (give or take five pills) the pathetically small number that was left in the bottle.

In my heart, I knew there was no escaping the resounding failure this 'attempt' had been. So I told him everything I took, including the Benylin, to which I think I caught him suppress a smile. He told us "I have to ring Guy's hospital with this information. They have a specialist drug research unit and they could tell us if any of those drugs could have a reaction in the body".

"InshAhllah" [God willing], I secretly hoped.

"Yes, my son is medical student there", Ami proudly stated.

The doctor smiled as he picked up his clipboard and left the room, clearly thinking, "Not all of your children are screw ups then".

Later that night, I was moved to the children's ward. I was given a single room to stay in overnight. It was decorated for a child and had a parent's bed in it. Ami slept in it that night. The hospital provided me with a gown and I changed into that for bed that night, rather than my normal shalwaar kameez.

The next day Ami went home to "get my pyjamas", but in fact went to Marks & Spencer's to buy me something 'decent' to sleep in instead. While she was gone, I remember complaining to a nurse that I was constipated, when she reminded me that we could probably put that down to the packet of Imodium that I had taken. I laughed, struck by how absurdly I had behaved. Then I filled in a BDI[84] form that the hospital had given me.

---

[84] The Beck Depression Inventory (BDI) is a 21-question multiple-choice self-report inventory, one of the most widely used instruments for measuring the severity of depression. Nowadays, though, it has been refined into the practice health questionnaire (PHQ 9). The introduction of the BDI in the 1960s marked a shift among health care professionals, who had tended to understand depression from patients' psychodynamic perspectives, instead of it being rooted in the patient's own thoughts.

After I had done all of this Ami still was not back. I worried about her. I was troubled by the thought that something awful had happened because she was thinking about the fact her daughter was in hospital. I lay in bed imagining the horrific and absurd scenarios that could have occurred. The reason for her "delay" was no more than a teenager's lack of ability to 'de-centre', realise that the world does not revolve around her and estimate an appropriate length of time for how long the bus takes.

Later, when she had returned and I had eaten my lunch, I was taken to a school on the children's ward. It was there to limit any disruptive effects that illness had on patients' education. I thought about the lessons I was missing and felt guilty for abandoning Katherine, my vegetarian lab partner, who had to dissect the sheep's heart all by herself.

The school was a large single room that had been blandly decorated. The magnolia walls were decorated with paintings, presumably by past students. They had been mounted on sugar paper and blu-taced to the walls. It also contained some other functional objects, such as a PC on a trolley. In the centre of the room there were some small tables pushed together to form a central work station, around which all the pupils sat.

I sat down on one of the small chairs next to the teacher, who was in turn sitting next to a teenage boy. He was white and looked a few years older than me.

"What are you in here with?" he asked.

"OD", I answered coolly, trying to dismiss it.

"Me too," he responded matter-of-factly.

I was a bit taken aback at how unashamed he seemed of this. He said that he had done it because he wanted to show his parents that he was not happy with their decision to move the family, after his father had found a new job.

"Why did you do it?" he asked me.

"I don't know", I said, before the teacher interrupted, telling him, "That's enough of that. Leave her alone." The boy's reason seemed very emotionally manipulative, and it has probably stuck in my mind because I knew that deep down I was just the same. So I was relieved as I watched him turn around.

Later that day I was seen by the consultant psychiatrist, Dr Sturge. She talked to me, Ami and Naveed: separately to begin with and then together. When I saw her by myself, at first I dismissed the "suicide attempt" as a pathetic effort. Then halfway through the consultation, I spoke to her less defensively, explaining that "Everyone would be better off without me."

When she asked me, "Don't you think they'd be sad to see you go?" I explained that, "Of course they would be, at first; but it's for the best in the long run." I went on to explain that people can get over bereavement, but people rarely overcome the sort of shame and disrepute I would bring on the family once I was grown up. "It's better for me to die now, before I grow up and they've had a chance to fall in love with me."

She was doubtless familiar with the mental health problems that second generation immigrants can have. In researching this book I have learnt that the problems are not exclusive to south Asian females, but all immigrant communities. [85] (And not just in Britain: it can also apply to Brits who have emigrated.) There is often a torn sense of identity that can come from the conflict in the messages that come from the home environment and wider society. Then, later, when we were all together, perhaps because of my attempted denial of the seriousness of the situation, she reminded us: "However we look at it: a young girl here took an overdose and actions to try and end her own life."

I'm not sure how true that is.

When Dr Sturge wrote out the prescription for Prozac, she explained the dosage, telling us that every morning and evening Ami should give me two tablets. She explained the weaning-on process and reassured her that this was from the modern range of anti-depressants, which were new on the market and did not have the same nasty side effects as tablets that doctors had to prescribe a decade earlier.

To reassure us, she added that these tablets were no more harmful than over-the-counter headache remedies, such as paracetamol (and we all had first-hand experience of how pathetic they were at causing harm). Then she advised Ami to supervise me swallowing the tablets, because young girls like me had been known to deviously save up their tablets over several months for an overdose.

---

[85] Care Quality Commission, 2009, *Count me in*. Results of the 2009 national census of inpatients on supervised community treatment in mental health and learning disability services in England and Wales.

In addition to this, I was offered a choice of two different types of talking therapy. The first was family-based and would work on how we could use my obviously very loving family to help me overcome my depression. The other option was one where I would work by myself to look at my personal psychology. Unsurprisingly, I opted for the latter. It was a form of Cognitive Behavioural Therapy (CBT) that was specially modified in order to meet the needs of children and adolescents.

Cognition, she explained, is how we process the information we get from our senses and use it to understand the world around us. This therapy would help me examine the way I see things and how it had paved the way for my suicidal feelings.

"Like when you say someone's got rose-tinted spectacles on," I said. "I guess I've got grey-tinted specs on. And this therapy will help me take those glasses off, and see the world like normal people do."

"Yes, you can think of it like that", she reassured me.

She referred me to Dr Glynn, a child psychiatrist, who would give me the CBT. It started with some assessment sessions, which helped Dr Glynn to start building some trust. It was in these sessions a door opened to my heart. For the first time in my life − or at least, for the first time in my adolescence − I was able to speak openly.

I had never, until now, had the opportunity to share the worries that plagued this over-achieving middle class teenager. Any close friendships that I had cultivated with girls from school were drowning in a sea of peer pressure: I was always pre-occupied with trying to appear less nerdy than I was. All the girls, who I knew through my family, had evolved in the shadow of community expectations. I knew that if I acted like the real me I would be cast as 'a coconut' (brown on the outside, but white inside).

I was never bullied into believing that someone should behave a certain way just because of the colour of their skin. But I knew that if I did not have the right taste in clothes, music and films, no 'auntie' would propose her son's hand in marriage − not to a girl who did not reflect our shared culture.

On Tuesday afternoons I had Latin and double PE after lunch, so that was when we arranged that I would see Dr Glynn. On the first Tuesday she just talked to me about my life. But in her homework task the real work started, and Dr Glynn tried to make me take off the grey-tinted spectacles that were starting to make a snug place for themselves on the front my face. She asked me to bring to the next session a list of three positive things about each member of my family. And the session after that, my homework was to write a similar list about myself. I cannot remember what I wrote for the first two points, but I distinctly remember the third: "I get rubbish grades, but if I went to a normal school I would be clever."

For my next homework, Dr Glynn asked me to write down some coping strategies that I could use when feeling low. We discussed them later, and she told me to look at this list whenever I felt frustrated or worthless. Instead of cutting myself, she said that I should turn to these strategies.

One of the strategies on this list was doing my homework. If I was feeling ultra-depressed, I had been advised to immerse myself in homework. At the end of the school year I had been feeling so dismal that I got straight As.

About a decade later, I no longer had any homework to distract myself with, so I had to remove my 'grey-tinted spectacles' all over again. Few depressives are ever 'cured of depression'. Often all that can be done is to help learn how to break the cycle that led them to this point, but the cycle is the depression. So if things go wrong, it can come back all over again.

11 Solutions

Saturday 3rd April 2010

I'm getting quite weirded out by all this memory loss stuff. Ben's take on events for the things I've forgotten just don't seem right. I'm not saying he's lying: it's just that it seems quite odd and out of character. So sometimes I think that "these must have been the first signs of the brain damage", but then I remember that this doesn't work like that.

I can't get my head round any of it. I remember him being the love of my life and always being SO honest with him and telling him ALL of my feelings. But now he seems to say things that don't fit with that.

I must have been deluding myself into believing that things were the way I thought they were. He says how we used to have crazy rows sometimes. And how he doesn't like me saying stuff, because it reminds him of when I used to nag him. I know that all women are nags, but I really thought that I was different.

Just little things, like when we're cooking and he wants to add a stock cube to the pan and he says, "You'd never have let me do that before." And I just think, "I never used to let you add an Oxo cube to some stew?!" The old Faiza must have been a real Nazi.

Later on I was talking to him about this "old Faiza" business, and we got onto all this memory stuff. He said that I should ask Suzy [my psychologist] to refer me to a counsellor.

***

I have since come to the conclusion that the "old Faiza" was not a Nazi. But Ben wasn't lying either. She was confident and his experience of her was someone who stated her opinions with what he saw as an excessive degree of confidence.

Famously, if you ask a room full of people for their memory of an event, there will be as many different stories as the number of people in the room. Everybody's experience of a time is individual. My ideas of how I behaved at that time have been lost. We can never get them back.

***

Wednesday 14th April 2010

I asked Suzy about being referred to a counsellor, like Ben said I should. It wasn't as straightforward as I thought it'd be. I THOUGHT it would be something like:

Me: I'm weirded out by all my memory loss. Can I be referred to a counsellor to help me come to terms with it?
Suzy: Hmmm... yeah.

And then she'd do the paperwork.

But it wasn't anything like that. We had to discuss it!

But I'm quite proud of myself: I thought on my feet and stood my ground. But, that doesn't mean that I got my way in the end though. She said, "Don't you get to talk about your feelings here?" I said, "I find that it's all a bit too solution-focussed. I think I might benefit from more of a counselling-style approach."

See how well judged that was? I used all the lingo: "solution-focussed" rather than saying "You just tell me what to do," and "I might benefit from...", instead of "What you need to do is ..." I didn't swear at her. Didn't shout, "You're so annoying, thinking you know what's in the best interests of this dumb-arse."

Anyway, she didn't pass me on to a counsellor. She said I should stick with her and she'd have a "more counselling style approach." I'll take that as "I had no idea that you were onto my case. I thought I could get away with just telling you what to do because, after all, I am the expert with head cases like you."

Friday 7th May 2010

... had a psychology session today. I was looking forward to it because Suzy said now the sessions would be all new look: with more of a "counselling-style approach". I thought she'd pull through and stop telling me what to do. But the session I had today looked remarkably similar to the old ones. Even I remembered, so that can't be her excuse.

Anyway, maybe I'll email her about getting referred. Email's better because then I don't have the danger of screaming, "Listen to me. Stop acting like you know better than me what's best for me."

Friday 14th May 2010

Suzy said that to be referred to a counsellor I need to go through my GP. She also said that I can't keep seeing her, because the NHS won't let me see her AND a counsellor.

Which I said was fair enough: trying not to look too delighted that I would never have to see this person again: someone who's an apparent expert on all head injuries everywhere.

So we went to see the GP. Ben came with me, because he's supposed to now. So, they've referred me to a counsellor, although there's a risk that they could do more harm than good. (Like those crap OTs.) I imagined they'd try and put me on pills as a quicker, cheaper fix, but they said they'd do a counsellor too.

I think Ben wants to palm me off to some sort of a therapist. I was saying that I'll probably never get to see a therapist anyway, but he reckons that I'm in with a good chance because of "my history" and this car crash. Why I can't talk about all this to the love of my life I don't understand, but I guess it's just too much for him. I guess I must be too crazy for a normal man to handle. After all, he is a man.

Not that I actually cry any more. I go to cry, but nothing happens. I don't think that I'm less upset than before. It just feels like my tear ducts are clogged. Mind you, the old Faiza had never been in this weird head-fucky situation before, so we don't know if she'd be "coping" like this or having a massive breakdown.

I have thought about cutting myself, because I need to have some sort of coping mechanism, and that one's tried and tested. But I think this situation's complicated enough without me caving into that one. I promised myself I wouldn't do that anymore when I was 13 and I won't go down that slippery slope.

***

Technically, I didn't cry on Ben's shoulder any more. This is not because there was something wrong with my tear ducts or because my life was easy. Injury to the brain can, unsurprisingly, affect a person's emotional processing.

The limbic system, also known as the reptilian brain, works at the core of the body's emotions. Damage to its cingulate cortex is associated with under-emotional behaviour in head injury survivors and an underactive basal ganglia (at the base of the fore brain) is associated with people who are not easily moved to tears. (Or alternatively, an overactive basal ganglia is associated with the excessive teariness associated with "normal" functioning.[86])

---

[86] Steele, J.C.; J. Richardson, J. C.; Olszewski, J. (1964). "Progressive Supranuclear Palsy. A Heterogeneous Degeneration Involving the Brain Stem, Basal Ganglia and Cerebellum With Vertical Gaze and Pseudobulbar Palsy, Nuchal Dystonia and Dementia." in Archives of Neurololgy 10(4):333-359

Although I was (and still am) affected by emotional lability, and was highly expressive of extreme emotions such as laughter or anger, I was also emotionally flat. Even though my emotions were not 'normal' anymore, I still had the massive task of understanding how my new brain works. And Ben was my sounding board.

True, I was not so quick to tears, but I still had feelings. Weren't they still as important?

***

Wednesday 9th June 2010

I had an appointment with this new consultant today[87]. We talked to him about how I do tick quite a few of their boxes on their depression questionnaire. But they're just all things that are symptoms of depression that coincide with the head injury. I wanted to ask him what we should make of all this.

Anyway, he gave me a prescription for some anti-depressants[88]. Ben says they put me on it before, when I was in the JR — he said that he asked them to prescribe me something after my "suicide attempt". Ami and Daddy reckon that I just fell out of my wheelchair. I hate to say it, but I think I agree with them.

Given "my history" (the teenage suicide attempt, not the falling out of my wheelchair attempt!), Dr Henderson-Slater reckons that we should be extra cautious in case something "does happen". He's given me a prescription and I want to get started on them before we go to Spain. They take a week to kick in, but we're off in a couple of days.

I don't feel that low, but Ben says he reckons that I do seem to be. I'm personally not that bothered, but I don't want to bring him down because I look like I am.

---

[87] The 'new consultant' that my previous neurologist, Professor Kischka, referred me to was Dr Henderson-Slater. He is another neurologist who works for the John Radcliffe hospitals. Because he worked as a psychiatrist before training in neurology, he takes an interest in problems with mood.

[88] He prescribed me the SSRI anti-depressant Citalopram.

Monday 14th June 2010

In Asturias. On holiday. We've rented out this cottage in the Spanish countryside. There's an absolutely beautiful view[89]. We have a little garden and earlier I was sitting out and I did a bit of sketching in my holiday sketch book. It's really lovely and peaceful here. I hardly ever get changed out of my jim-jams. We go for little walks on some days (but it's not all paradise, I do have to get dressed on those days!).

These pills have reduced my so-called anxiety and have made me chill out. In fact, I'm so chilled that all I can do is sleep. I think I preferred being unchilled. But that was at the cost of being awake forever!

The house is quite fun. They've got a few DVDs. It's not a great selection, but it doesn't really matter because even slobbing out in front of the TV is too much for me sometimes.

Monday 22nd June 2010

I've stopped taking the pills. I'm kind of glad to be pill-free. It's not that I think there's any shame in it, but there's something about not being ill anymore. I am a bit sick of being sick. I know neurological damage is slow to repair, but this is ridiculous. I wanted to stop while we were in Spain, but I didn't dare risk it while we were out there, because I couldn't be bothered with any issues.

But I was telling Wendy about it and she said that coming off's never an issue; you only ever need to wean ONTO them...

Tuesday 6 July 2010

I've been seeing this counsellor at the GP's surgery. Her name's Irina and she's really nice. Just what I need. Someone who listens to ME and doesn't have some weird obsession with

---

[89] I would not have remarked on "the view", but it seemed important to Ben, which is why I mentioned it. I was unable to admit this to myself, but we were essentially there for him, to relax and recuperate. I was acutely aware how my illness had made the last year and a half stressful for him. He never said it to me, in fact he even put on a brave face – but even with my impaired social judgement, I could read the signs. Whenever I tried to talk to my friends about how I had inflicted this hard time upon him, I would immediately be dismissed, because it seemed preposterous to outsiders that I thought the injury was a great burden on him. The head injury, after all, did happen to my head. I often beat off friends who'd mistakenly leap to my defence, joking that, "I was too brain damaged to know what was going on. So, how *could* it have been harder for me?" My existence was dominated by feelings of guilt that I had for acquiring a brain injury, and having thrust the role of 'carer' onto the man I love.

grading me as a person. She sees past these "functional impairments" that seem to blind everyone else. In fact, she even gets me cups of tea[90]!!

I talked to her a bit about suicide (being careful to not go into details, being all too aware that if she suspected, she would have no choice but to break confidentiality and "take further action"). I was telling her about the other day, when I only got out of bed because someone had to go downstairs to open the conservatory door for the cats (poor Blackypuss needs her morning Go Cat). Before, I guess, I just used to get out of bed because I knew I had to – or there would be no one to take the register for 9F. But now I get paid simply for being disabled, what's the point?

I joked "The only reason I got out of bed was for a cat!" She didn't laugh. And I don't think it's because she doesn't "do irony". I think she deliberately didn't laugh in order to not validate the fact that my life is now pointless. I think she was trying to say "if a cat gives you meaning, then that's where you find meaning." But shouldn't I have meaning for myself, and not have to rely on a cat? And what if Blackypuss gets run over?

Then I said to her "I know you can't tell me just like that, but I have been asking myself 'what is the meaning of life?'" She said she'd lend me a book! [91] Hope it's not Hitch Hiker's Guide to the Galaxy!

Then I talked about my apparent suicide attempt in the John Radcliffe and how I might have been onto something: that there might not be a point to life now that I'm crippled.

---

[90] I often joked about how OTs are obsessed with assessing you by asking you to make a cup of tea. Through making a cup of tea the OT can assess a number of skills (including: orientation in the environment, ability to plan, staying focused in order to complete the task, memory of the correct sequence of making the tea; and physical aptitudes including posture, the ability to reach and locate objects).

[91] The book Irina ultimately lent me was Viktor Frankl's *In Search Of Meaning*. Frankl was an Austrian neurologist and psychiatrist who survived the Holocaust. *In Search Of Meaning* chronicles his time in a concentration camp and describes his psychotherapeutic method of finding meaning in all forms of existence. He uses his experience to tackle a question that many of us face: the meaning of existence. Frankl was one of the key figures in existential psychotherapy. He was the founder of a form of existential analysis, logotherapy, and wrote about how a sense of purpose and a desire to live is often derived from a feeling that one's life is purposeful. Frankl gave his patients voluntary work to do, in order to help them find meaning in their lives.

She said that what I'm going through is similar to mourning, but I'm mourning the loss of abilities. She said that the whole thing's a grieving process. [92]

I know that so many people would do anything to be in my position, so I feel like there must be something wrong with me: I can't even be happy getting paid for doing nothing all day.

Friday 16 July 2010

Ben showed me this Powerpoint presentation that they gave at Headway. It said that depression is quite common for head cases. Obviously, for some people the head injury itself is quite a traumatic thing, but there are weird biological things to do with it too, apparently.

I'm never hungry and I can't sleep so it does sound like depression, but I don't really feel depressed! All that stuff is just because of the head injury. So it's not proper depression.

Most head cases complain about the fatigue, but I should be so lucky! At least then there'd be fewer hours to endure. When I was in the OCE I used to sleep all the time, but now I just can't. I go to bed, just to lie there but I just can't fall asleep. I lie there awake. In bed. At least then I'm resting.

It happens so much these days that I've started taking my iPod to bed with me: I can listen to it with the volume on low, so I don't disturb B. I get loads of interesting radio 4 podcasts delivered to it[93]. I think that there's no point in just lying there, I might as well do something useful.

B reckons that we should go and talk to the GP. Maybe they'll give me some sleeping pills. But he reckons that I could have depression, so no doubt they will try and force some happy pills on me. I don't think there's any shame in them, but what fails to go into his head is that I don't have that all-important symptom: feeling depressed. OK, I do feel a bit sad sometimes (but who doesn't? And don't I have a right to: I have been in this "traumatic event"). But I hate the way normal feelings that aren't "happy, happy, happy" are held against me to prove some kind of point.

---

[92] Irina was referring to the Kubler Ross model of bereavement, which has often been applied to people who face loss in their lives, such as divorce, acquiring a disability or coping with redundancy.

[93] I did not have podcasts delivered directly to my iPod. At this time I was not able to sync my iPod with my laptop, so Ben would download some appropriate podcasts and transfer them to my iPod for me. Although I was aware that he did this, I was unable to decentre sufficiently in order to articulate this sufficiently to myself. For quite a long time, this is how I would think about the mechanics of everyday life.

It kind of annoys me that people think that I SHOULD be depressed because of this car crash. Then they all act like I'm in denial when I say that I'm fine. When I act as though I'm happy they think "How can she be?" But I really am.[94] I've had depression before and this doesn't compare.

But Ben uses that against me and says that with my "history", we should be extra cautious and act on the first signs, before it's "too late".

***

The Powerpoint presentation that Ben showed me was one that accompanied a talk for carers given by the brain injury charity Headway. It explained how survivors of head injuries can often suffer from depression. In any particular case no one can isolate a single reason for this. The victim might have to look for new employment or there could be turbulence to existing relationships, which makes victims more susceptible to depression and anxiety. Survivors also need to learn how their new brain works in a society filled with myths and misconceptions about brain damage. Some of the symptoms can also be explained by damage to the pineal gland.

The pineal gland controls production of the neurotransmitter serotonin and a reduced production of it is associated with depression. Even though it is not actually a hormone, it is often called the "happiness hormone" and some studies have shown that serotonin can also affect memory and concentration. What can be said confidently is that serotonin is a chemical neurotransmitter associated with feelings of well-being.

The problems I had looked largely biological: I had poor appetite and problems sleeping. (If I slept at all, I would manage a maximum of 4 hours sleep in a night.) [95] As far as I was concerned, I could not sleep because of some mysterious aspect of my brain's chemistry, that anyone who was not a neuroscientist could not

---

[94] I think that any feelings of anxiety and depression were unable to manifest themselves in feelings of worry. Neurological damage from my head injury had made me emotionally numb. And my introspective intelligence had been reduced to the point that I could not identify the feelings that were building up inside me. So although I clearly had depression, I did not think that I was depressed.

[95] I probably did manage to get some sleep – people often complain of a 'sleepless night', when they did in fact sleep. The brain might not register that it is asleep if it only enters stage 1 sleep. Stage 1 sleep refers to the initial stages of sleep and lasts for 5-10 minute periods.

understand. And my reduced appetite could only be a good thing, while the majority of the UK population was obese or overweight; I had never been so slim.

***

Because I had stopped taking the Citalopram after just a week, my GP wrote me out another SSRI anti depressant, Venlafaxine, which he garnished with heavy advice to persevere with them, because apparently the side effects would die down after the first few weeks:

Tuesday 28 September 2010

Yesterday we went to see the GP about my "depression". He said that the council are processing my counselling referral and I have to wait till that comes through. Being a GP, he had to try and push me some "uppers". You hear about how they give out happy pills like they're smarties, but I had no idea it was to this extent. I'm not even that sad. Well, obviously I've been through this "traumatic, life changing event", but I think I'm still fairly stable. I'd say I'm coping pretty well, in fact. But bizarrely I don't think that's allowed in our society today: they've gone from "depression's nothing to be ashamed of" to "coping is prohibited".

So, Dr Brown asked me a bit about where I'm at with all these depression therapies (both pills and "talking therapies"). I told him about how I only took the Citalopram for a week because of the [side effect of] fatigue. So, he prescribed some other anti-depressants! He told me to make sure I persevere with these ones because the side effects would die down after the first few weeks.

The tablets are best taken with food, so I had them with my dinner. Then about an hour after taking them I noticed that I was grinding my teeth and getting MILD jaw pain. Ben read the leaflet that they came with and noticed that it had advice "to seek immediate medical advice if I have any of the following symptoms" and one of them was jaw pain! But, by this time it was 7 in the evening and the GP would be shut. And the only place I could possibly get to see a doctor was A&E!

I thought this was a stupid idea! Especially when Ben had to be in the office today. So he came up with the idea of phoning NHS direct. They said I shouldn't have started with a full dose, and that I should cut the tablets in half, gradually wean myself onto them and go and see the GP the next day. So, I went to bed.

As I lay there I began to think, "That Dr Brown laid it on quite thick about how I should persevere with the venlafaxine regardless of the side effects." Gradually this became "Ah well, that's just what he wants you to do" and then I began to think "How can I even know I've got a head injury?"

After all, there isn't much physical evidence of it, and I only have people's word for the fact that my brain wasn't working properly. They could have just invented all these events that I've "forgotten". They could easily engineer the few occasions I do have a sense that something's wrong with my brain. They could have briefed people to act in the right way around me and stick to some sort of vague script.

I do think it has all been really good for Ben. He's been getting the upper-hand with everything since the accident. It was all a giant conspiracy from the white world: "they" (Ben, the doctors etc.) had worked together to stop this young Asian teacher, who was becoming quite successful in brainwashing "our" [white] children in her "brown" ways.

Ben's family had always seemed to resent the fact that their own flesh and blood had fallen in love with a Paki. They never said it explicitly, but now I look back I can definitely sense there was something there.[96] All I can say is that it's all a bit too 'convenient' how I can't be a teacher because of some reason that I couldn't possibly understand.

And I seem to remember that I was quite a good teacher. They could allow this to happen in some Camden comprehensive, which was full of immigrants. But at some posh little private school, I heavily suspect that this wasn't the case. It's full of the offspring of the actual people who had organised this "head injury".

After a few minutes of following this avenue of thought, it rang a bell that in the Venlafaxine leaflet, where it mentioned all the side effects, I remembered it saying something about "paranoid delusions".

It occurred to me that the Venlafaxine manufacturers (who printed the leaflet that listed the side effects) could be a part of the 'white society' that had been conspiring against me, because they had foreseen that the tablets could lift the veil from my eyes and let me see the truth of what was going on. They wanted me to dismiss my new insight as mere "paranoid delusion".

---

[96] I perhaps need to underline that the idea that I had racist in-laws is something that I wrote in my own private diary, after suffering a drug-induced paranoid delusion. I know that this is not at all what Ben's family thought of me. They have actually been very accepting and have welcomed me into their home.

I remember when I was a teenager, I thought that paranoia had within it elements of arrogance: only an arrogant person thinks they are so special, that everyone is after them. But then I remembered that Nirvana lyric, "Just because you're paranoid, don't mean we're not after you."

So I think I'll wait till Ben gets home, and see what he thinks, but after what Dr Brown said about persevering with the tablets despite the side effects I reckon I could stay on them. But I think if I just take half tablets and wean myself onto them like NHS direct said I should, I reckon I'll be alright.

***

I find it a little deflating to learn that the thoughts I had can be explained by biochemistry...

The reason I had these delusions was because something went wrong with the venlafaxine. Venlafaxine works by inhibiting the reuptake of serotonin; what this means in practice is that it increases the levels of serotonin in the brain.

We can't be sure, but it looks like this was a case of serotonin syndrome, which is an adverse reaction to anti-depressants.[97] Although having enough serotonin is essential to having a healthy brain, too much of it can be toxic. An excess of serotonin would explain the delusional experience of making wacky connections. Pumped up with serotonin, my brain linked up my experiences of brain injury with my life circumstances around the car crash. I made associations between my circumstances and the sort of person I perceived myself to be, as a result of this arbitrary neurochemical change.

Although I have no proof, I can dismiss these thoughts as delusional ones... or is that just what they want you to think?!

---

[97] Some German psychiatrists have reported a similar case involving a 37 year-old woman who experienced hallucinations after being given venlafaxine.

Ebert, D. & Klein, T. 'Hallucinations as a side effect of venlafaxine treatment - a case report', in *Psychiatry On-line*. Retrieved 30/09/2013.

12 Growing Up

By the end of year 11, I managed to score the good crop of GCSEs that the school demanded of students if they wanted to stay on for sixth form. It had been years since I last wanted to cut myself. The coping strategy of immersing myself in my studies, whenever I was feeling down, had woven itself into my personality – to the extent I was singled out as one of the bright sparks, who should be encouraged to apply to Cambridge (or Oxford).

There are millions of reasons why I was cautious of such an institution. My gut told me that "People like us don't go to Cambridge". I also knew that it was a high-pressured institution which was not advisable for someone with my history of depression. Ami never liked the idea because I would have to live away from home. But I went, reassuring her that she could trust me.

Then while I was there, I met Ben. We were friends, that was as far as it went, but now our friends tell us it was blatantly obvious to bystanders that something was going to happen; it had become a weekly occurrence that we would fall to the back of the group on our long walk back to college from the student night at Cindy's. [98]

As our graduation date drew closer, I worried constantly about the impending tragedy for which I would be responsible - my family's disappointment. I decided that I would postpone my doom and apply to do a year's teacher training to be a science trainer. There were two massive advantages to this. First, I could stay in Cambridge another year. Second, I would probably walk into a job anywhere in the country because physics teachers, especially female ones, were a rare commodity. (This was essential because I had no idea how things would work out with my family once I told them about Ben; I needed to have access to enough funds to feed myself, and probably Ben, no matter what happened.)

---

[98] Cindy's is the name of a dingy club that had their student night every Tuesday. (This was the same evening that Selwyn College held its 'Formal Hall'.)

When it came to the crunch, my family's disappointment was not in the same league as the horror stories that media reports had led me to believe were the norm amongst the crazy Muslim families inhabiting every corner of our civilised nation. They did not attend our registry office ceremony –probably because they were given less than a week's notice for their only daughter's proud day. But they did throw a feast 6 months later.

***

Gradually things got better: my relationship with my crazy Muslim parents began to settle; Ben and I moved into a nicer flat, and I changed schools. I have really fond memories of teaching in Camden. The kids were no angels. They weren't devils either. They were just kids. Some good. Many annoying. Every one of them different. I loved it. At least I think I did.

And the icing on the cake was that I really felt at home in London. I loved the way it was grimy. The way you'd blow your nose after a day in the city and have a tissue that was filled with grey bogie.

Ben hated it. He is not at all nostalgic for this urban dumping ground. My old emails from him are filled with references to his desire to escape from the concrete landscape. We made the deal that we would pay for me to do an MA at a London University and then move somewhere nice. And that's what we did.

I did an MA in science education, then I got a job in Oxford. We traded in our grubby little North London flat for a converted barn in a village outside Oxford. I had only been there a term when I was involved in a serious car crash.

My life changed. Our lives changed.

13 Paranoid?

Wednesday 22nd September 2010

I had another appointment today with Dr Brown today, just to talk a bit more about the Venlafaxine stuff. I was telling him how it sometimes feels like aliens have taken over my brain[99] and he said that paranoia is a common side effect of many neurological conditions[100] and he wants to be sure this is actually from the Venlafaxine.

I'm finding this all quite frustrating. Why can't I just see him as 'Faiza Siddiqui'? I'm always Faiza 'victim of a traumatic brain injury' Siddiqui. Why can't the doctors see past all these destroyed neurones? They just seem so intent on saying my 'low mood' is a direct result of this bang on the head. Then they come up with some complicated part of the brain it must have destroyed.

***

As the weeks went by I began to feel that my ideas about 'white society' plotting against my success could probably be explained away as a paranoid delusion caused by the Venlafaxine. Although the pills triggered my brain to make connections, these thoughts were definitely constructed against the background of a modern capitalist society, or what people sometimes call 'the man'. Although I am cautious of attaching too much Freudian baggage to this, the idea must have come from somewhere.[101]

---

[99] The feeling that "aliens have taken over my brain" probably stems from a disconnected sense of being. In *Illness* Havi Carel discusses a question that everyone faces: mortality. With both emotional honesty and philosophical rigour, she examines the alienation that everyone has from their imperfect bodies and the exacerbation of this feeling by illness or disability. She writes about how for her the question of mortality, that she studied academically, was turned upside-down when she had to live with terminal lung cancer.

[100] Paranoia is associated with damage to the amygdala, the almond shaped group of nuclei located in the brain's medial temporal lobes.

[101] The idea that "this must have come from somewhere" was probably influenced by what the old Faiza had read about anti-psychiatry. Anti-psychiatry was a movement that started in the 1960s that challenged many of psychiatry's most fundamental assumptions and practices, and which sought to develop more humane alternatives to them. Its most influential writer, R.D. Laing, focused particularly on the actual experience of psychosis. Laing's views on the causes and treatment of serious mental dysfunction were greatly influenced by his reading of existential philosophy, and ran strongly against the grain of the psychiatric orthodoxy of

As well as indulging in a bit of self-analysis, I asked myself the question "How would I act differently if white society had constructed the illusion of this injury?" The answer was simple; I would take more steps to return to work. But could it be too much hassle for them to re-employ me? Would they rather just give me the sack? Surely they couldn't - there must be laws against it.

The school constantly reassured me that "my job is open for my return", always adding eagerly (a bit too eagerly, if you ask me) that there is no pressure from them to return to work before I'm ready. They would leave it to me to say when I felt that I was ready. This was frustrating, because I was ready. The only thing stopping me returning to work was Ben's opinion that "I was not ready yet". Exactly what was wrong with me, he could never explain.

Now, when I see in-patients at the OCE (when I go there for voluntary work), I am no better at articulating exactly the ways in which they are impaired. Saying "there's just something wrong with you", I have learnt, is not the right thing to say, although it does capture the vagueness of its presentation.

I mentioned to my OTs (at the OCE) my intention to return to work soon. They were not encouraging. They acted surprised and never saw it as the sensible choice. Much of the advice on the internet seemed to say the same. But it seemed there were no black-and-white answers when it came to head injuries. All that could be said is "well, it depends on the case". This did little to alleviate my paranoia.

Although it cut against my nature to demonstrate patience, they successfully conned me into believing that it would do no harm to wait and might actually be in my best interests. So I reluctantly concluded that I should wait before returning to work. I felt that these ideas about 'white society' conspiring against me could, at least in part, be explained as an unwanted side effect of the Venlafaxine.

---

his day by taking the expressed feelings of the patient as valid descriptions of lived experience, rather than simply as symptoms of some separate underlying disorder or disease-process. Politically, he was regarded as a thinker of the New Left who saw psychosis as a sane response to an insane capitalist society.

In fact, I started to see the funny side of this whole episode, smugly maintaining that the whole event was a useful window into my subconscious. I boasted how "other people would pay hundreds of pounds for months of psychoanalysis to get this - I got it for the price of a prescription." Perhaps an analogy could be made with psychologist Timothy Leary's[102] use of hallucinogenic drugs to open up the mind.

***

A year and a bit, after my discharge from the OCE, the new academic year had started and it had been exactly a decade since starting University at Selwyn College. We went up for a special reunion dinner. I have extremely fond memories of this event and my diary entries probably would not present a reliable picture of it. So, here is a diary entry I have written based on a combination of my diary, emails and vague memories:

Monday 27 September 2010

We had the Selwyn College 10 year reunion last Saturday. I had a really good time. I don't think anyone else was as excited as I was: they all get out a bit more! It just felt kind of good to be a student for the weekend and re-live the glory of the old Faiza: be a clever Cambridge student without actually having to use my brain.

Typical us, we got up late and had to leave the house in a crazy hurry. I do feel bad because I'm not as undisabled as I used to be and can't just grab all the last minute stuff that we hadn't bothered to pack the night before. I'd never have neatly packed a bag before, so I'm a bit resentful that I'm supposed to now.

I'd have been quite happy to grab a pair of pants, toothbrush and my going out shoes as I ran to the car on my way out. But I can't do that anymore: I have so much more paraphernalia now[103], I can't carry as much and I always forget stuff. And I certainly can't run out to the car. Everything about me is just a bit crapper (and slower).

---

[102] Timothy Leary was an American psychologist and writer, known for his advocacy of psychedelic drugs for therapeutic reasons. Leary believed LSD showed therapeutic potential for use in psychiatry and popularized catchphrases such as "turn on, tune in, drop out" that promoted his philosophy.

[103] The "paraphernalia" that I needed to take with me included a variety of items: antibiotic cream that I had to apply daily, which was prescribed for the acne that I got as a result of

And because of my memory and the fact that being organised was my department before, we forgot our air mattress. I had it all planned out, how we could smuggle it in without alerting the [college] porters.

What we'd do is smuggle it in its deflated form, covered with a coat. Then we could take it to our ground floor room (we knew it'd be ground floor because Ben asked for a special cripple room for me) and inflate it through the window using that camping pump we have that goes in the car cigarette lighter. We could park the car right outside college, because we could use my disabled badge. I had it all planned out, but then we forgot the air mattress! So Ben and I had to share a single bed.

But, it still felt good to reminisce about student days. There was an afternoon tea. Then dinner. I resented paying something like £80 for a formal hall that used to cost us a fiver back in the day. I was complaining to everyone about how overpriced it was, but they all said that this dinner was in a different league to old formal halls. So it was all quite nice, apparently. I couldn't really see the difference though. [104] Wine was included, so no-one was smuggling in the illegal[105] stuff.

---

my body being under stress during rehab; diprobase cream prescribed for my legs, because damage to my pituitary gland caused my skin to become dry and itchy; tablets of gabapentin prescribed by my neurologist to prevent seizures, control neuropathic pain and hot flushes. As well as my various medicines, I would always carry a bottle of water. I needed to drink more water in order to prevent headaches, with are common to head injury victims, again because of neurological damage to the pituitary gland.

In addition I used to carry my filofax with me everywhere I went. It was like a security blanket and I could use it to look up dates and phone numbers that the 'old Faiza' would have just remembered. People often asked me "Why don't you just get a smart phone?", but I would be too ashamed to explain how I would struggle to teach myself to successfully navigate any sort of new technology, no matter how much it was marketed as 'idiot proof'. I also took my iPod if I was staying anywhere overnight, so that I could listen to it quietly to pass the time when my body should be sleeping. Listening to music with the volume down low would help keep me be calm(er) and prevent me from fidgeting in bed. The old-Faiza always used to boast about her "excellent bed-fellowship skills". It now became a joke between us that by crashing the car I had 'single-handedly' (with my unaffected upper limb) brought about the downfall of these skills. I would be a restless bed partner, often spending hours awake fidgeting, always too tired to get up and adjust the bedding that was causing me such irritation. All the while I would tell myself that "at least I'm resting".

[104] I felt that I could not, and probably really did not, enjoy the meal as much as the 'old Faiza' would have done. Damage to the parietal lobes affects sensory information received by the brain. This includes information about temperature, taste, touch, and movement from the rest of the body. This can result in the survivor's appreciation of the finer sensual pleasures of life being affected. Enjoyment of a fine meal can be significantly affected.

In *Season To Taste*, Molly Birnbaum writes about her experience of hyposmia (loss of sense to smell). She was training as a chef, before her brain injury, and researched the sense that

After dinner the master gave a speech saying we should all remember Selwyn College in our wills! Just to rub it in that they do this reunion thing, not because they love us as part of the Selwyn family, but because we're now one of the college's cash cows. But I guess we just have to put up with them trying to squeeze money-milk out of our teats, as we bask in the blissful memories of student days.

I worried needlessly yet again. [106] *On this occasion, I worried that I wouldn't be able to remember my way back to our room after going to the loo in the middle of the night. I haven't got a dick, so I wouldn't be able to piss in the sink if I needed to.* [107] *I took a plastic jug with me so if I woke up needing a wee, I could kneel and put it between my legs and it would be a commode. Every room has a sink, so I would have a flushable commode!*

But Ben had got us a disabled room, because he had put it in my name. The whole emergency make-shift commode was unnecessary because it was a PROPER en suite! Despite the luxurious room, I slept REALLY badly, even for me nowadays. There were quite a few reasons behind this: 1. I was convinced that Ben was "bed hogging", because I forgot that we were squeezed into a college single. 2. Maybe because I wasn't in my normal bed and 3. I was a bit over-excited at being back at Selwyn.

Then the next morning, at breakfast, I think I was incredibly hyperactive. [108] *I sat next to Alex after getting myself a giant complimentary breakfast that Ben could have the*

---

she lost. So, after her injury, she wrote about how a sense of smell is a central aspect of human existence.

[105] Students who chose to bring their own bottle of wine to formal hall at Selwyn College, would be charged a fee for "corkage". At least when I was there, the students resented paying this additional fee, because they saw it as nothing more than college's money making scheme, charging students for simply for bringing their own wine. Students would normally open it before going to the dinner hall and smuggle it in hidden under a jacket, for example. I think we used to take pleasure in flaunting the pettiness of such rules and called such wine "illegal".

[106] I often worried needlessly. Studies have shown that patients, who have been the victim of a brain injury can have anxiety disorders, which can in part be explained by changes to the survivors' circumstances. Biological changes to the brain, specifically damage to the hippocampus, have also been associated with anxiety. Survivors are also faced with the task of learning to manage a new brain: a brain that functions significantly differently from both the pre-injury brain and from a 'normal' brain.

[107] Urinating into the sink was Ben's standard method for "going to the toilet" in the night. Amongst our friends he was often teased that he had an en suite for the price of a single room.

[108] I was, perhaps, especially hyperactive because of damage to my brain's prefrontal cortex. This can affect a person's ability to control their emotions. Generally speaking the frontal

majority of. Ben said that Al was a bit hung-over and I don't think I was the best breakfast partner for him. I got the impression from what he was saying that I was acting EXTREMELY hyper, talking really fast. Well, I was quite full on - my brain was going at 100 mph.

Anyway, we all then went out for lunch in town. I feel like I have the best friends in the world. They're all so understanding about my "disability". Like, I couldn't walk to town because I was so tired and they didn't ladle out pity. Then, when I was coming out of the Wetherspoons (ah, student days!), I was chatting to Fran. I was quite tired, and I think a bit disinhibited. I told her at length various toilet-related stories: annoyed because I had a giant wedgy and lamenting how I never got the opportunity to use my makeshift commode. She was so kind and just listened nicely without making any jokes at my expense, even though I'm sure she could think of loads!

I was SOOO exhausted by the time we made it home. It felt like my recovery went back at least a year. But no, it doesn't work like that. I was inhabiting my 'recovered' body, but it had crazy, impairment -shit smeared all over it. I felt car sick - way worse than I used to when I was taken across from the JR to the OCE. When we got off the M40 I was actually retching all the way home. [109]

***

Monday 4th October 2010

Sometimes I feel like God himself has willed this whole thing. It's all a little "convenient" how this head injury seems to be perfectly matched to my strengths. And it is a little too convenient how it was me who was the victim and Ben who was the carer: not the other way round. I'm definitely the tougher one. And Ben's too fussy to make a good patient.

---

lobes have a NO or STOP function, which can be especially affected if the subject is distracted or tired.

[109] Travel sickness is a common complaint for survivors of head injuries. Although its severity has decreased with time, it is always worse if I am tired. It can also be worsened by having something on my mind: it need not be worry, it might simply be if I am experiencing something new. An unfamiliar nuance on the feeling of happiness, for example, might require my brain to process a different set of feelings. This makes it harder to process the sensory inputs associated with motion, resulting in travel sickness. It is not the familiar sort of travel sickness: it is more a feeling of extreme tiredness: an inability to concentrate on the most basic tasks and withstand any kind of sensory input as well as the more familiar symptoms of travel sickness. This was probably the most travel sick I have felt, although I was never able to actually produce any vomit. I was retching from the M40, which is in fact only a mile or two from our house: about 5 minutes' drive along a country lane. Although it is not especially winding, it did make me feel more car sick than being on the straight motorway.

But he did make an excellent carer because he has some kind of gift for imagining things from other people's perspectives.

At CRG [cognitive rehabilitation group] they told me about how after head injuries people can become more spiritual and 'find God'. Maybe this is my way of doing it?

Friday 8*th* October 2010

I'm not quite sure what to make of what's going on in my head right now. Should I be worried? Make an appointment with the GP? But the last thing you should do if you're worried about being paranoid is go to the doctor: you're just asking to be locked up.

I just emailed Chris saying that I had such a lovely time at Selwyn and then I paranoidly thought "don't write that: the [Selwyn College] master will see it and target you for money for college". I thought that he taps into our emails, kind of like MI5. I only properly thought this for about 5 seconds before I was struck by how deeply insane it was. Am I being paranoid, or is that just what they want you to think?

And I do kind of feel like my body's being controlled by someone that's not me, like in Being John Malkovich. [110] And there are these scars all over my body where apparently some medical tube went in, or they did some procedure. Any one of them could be where they planted a chip in my head. That's why I have such shitty control over my body, because the impulses going down my nerves interfered with the signal from this chip. [111]

I dismissed this almost immediately, knowing how crazy it sounds. But what would I do differently if what I thought was true and not just the concoction of some paranoid nut case? Well, I'd do more to try and go back to work. At the moment Martin [the headmaster at my school] said there's no pressure from him to return to work, it's all 'when I feel ready'. Well, I feel ready now.

Yeah, it all sounds very "nice", but what's his real motive? Does he just want to appear as though he's a nice, supportive employer, while he works behind the scenes to put me off

---

[110] Being John Malkovich (1999) was a Charlie Kaufman film. It tells the story of some office workers who discover a portal which leads literally into the head of movie star John Malkovich, who plays the film's lead role. By entering this portal they can live, feel and experience whatever he does. As the film develops, the characters learn to control Malkovich's body — just as I felt I was learning to control my body again.

[111] The idea of my body being controlled by a Bluetooth chip is probably a response to the accelerated rate of technological advances that I experienced as a result of the amnesia. With the increased use of the internet and mobile technology, the world seemed to exist in a new technological age. With my memory loss, this seemed to have happened overnight.

being a teacher? It's all very suspicious. They're the caring employers, but still have this benefit to stop disabled people going back to work.

Technically the only thing stopping me is Ben. He says that it's a bad idea and he doesn't think that I can manage it. And every time I ask him why, he's all vague. I think I'm going to get that cognitive assessment thing, and he won't be able to argue with that.

I don't really think that he has got it in for me. I did, lying in bed that night. But now, I just reckon that he's being a scaredy cat about losing this disability insurance money. I don't think teaching will be a problem for me. It's not like teaching was at the limit of my cognitive abilities before anyway. [112] So, a little knock to the head might have put me back a bit, but I hope I can still be a science teacher: it's not like it was rocket science anyway.

***

It seems that the Venlafaxine side effect triggered some delusions: I started to feel as though God himself had micromanaged this whole incident. I started to think, "It's all a bit too convenient how this 'tragedy' was almost exactly suited to my strengths. It's almost as if someone from above had guided it." On some level, I still believe this, but I do appreciate that God is not as human as this seems to suggest.

One of my strengths is that I can be determined (Ami calls it being stubborn), which was an invaluable quality for rehabilitation from a severe brain injury. [113] I

---

[112] Any question about teaching falling "within my cognitive abilities" is an unfairly phrased one, because it does not allow for a sufficiently broad definition of intelligence.

Broadly speaking, psychologists , fall into one of two camps, when describing intelligence: generalists or localisers. Generalists see intelligence as a global thinking activity: if someone excels in visual-spatial thinking, they also tend to have a lot of linguistic intelligence. Localisers tend to see the different forms of intelligence as broadly unrelated. (Perhaps most famous localiser is Howard Gardener, with his controversial theory of multiple intelligences.) Cognitive ability tends to refer to a global form of intelligence, which we tend to see as 'cleverness'.

My ability to process information under specific circumstances would have affected my ability to teach. But, one of the biggest challenges that the people I knew faced, was to describe exactly how I was cognitively affected. The difficulty was not simply that my impairments were 'subtle'; it was that there was no single word that could describe the complex way in which my thinking had been affected. The only words that came close were either technical neuropsychological terms, which never really spoke to me; or they were words, such as concentration, that had been already been hijacked by the able-brained population. Essentially there were a number of 'subtle' cognitive impairments that would have affected my teaching.

[113] Although it is hard for me to admit this, the determination that I had, was probably not the most significant factor in my rehabilitation. A patient's rehabilitation from a neurological

was the one who needed to toil at the arbitrary tasks of rehabilitation, striving for the paltry reward of being praised as a good girl. It seemed like I was constantly being congratulated for minor achievements in a rehab that was itself unnecessary. But I did not feel patronised, like any normal human being might. Thriving as I did on the authority and praise of the able-bodied population, I was spurred on to dedicate myself to ever more exhausting, pointless tasks.

What is more, I had taken an MA in education because the nerd in me thought that it would be a fun way to spend a year. It seemed very convenient that I had learnt things like how best to manipulate people to allow them to learn. I studied this, or so I thought, to learn how teachers can tailor their lessons to best meet children's needs; little did I know that I would later apply these strategies on myself to help me understand how my new brain worked. Ben, on the other hand, would never have been so studious a patient, but made an excellent carer because of his incredible ability – I call it a gift, but he doesn't like it – for imagining experiences from another person's perspective.

I imagined that if I were a close friend of this girl who had just who had just come out of hospital with a serious head injury, and who started having bizarre paranoid delusions involving the Almighty, then I would advise her to go and see a professional. So, I decided to raise Dr Brown's concerns with my consultant. I explained to him how my GP thought that the paranoia could be a symptom of the head injury. "While I appreciate that the paranoia is not affecting my functioning at this stage," I told him, "I am concerned that it may be a problem if we don't nip it in the bud." I was careful to use the vocabulary of the medical world: 'functioning'. 'Functioning' dominated the lexicon of neuro-rehabilitation, because this was virtually the only sphere in which medical professionals could set objectively measurable targets.

Then as a joke I added, "What could be the possible consequences of this if we allowed it to escalate? Could we have another Waco on our hands?" Waco was a carefully chosen example. I wanted to refer to the potential of me becoming a suicide bomber if this were allowed to escalate, but Ben advised me that it probably would not be a wise choice, what with me being a Muslim and the nature of the paranoid delusion. Not that people would think I might actually blow myself up; it would just have added a further possibility for friction between me and my

---

condition is, to a significant extent, random. Of course, the patient's health, age and stimulation do play a role, but the body is its own master and no one can predict what the outcome will be. Patients can find it hard to believe that our 'recovery' is largely unrelated to the dedication we have put in; but many believe that it is.

doctor. I could not trust my own social judgement, so I chose to adopt the more white-person-friendly example of Waco instead.

Dr Henderson-Slater told me that I did not seem at all paranoid, reassuring me that he used to work as a psychiatrist and so had some experience of these matters. I told him that I already knew this because I had googled him when I heard I was being referred to him. He smiled, as though making a mental note of how this serves as a wonderful example of the localised nature cognitive impairments.

14 The Meaning of Life

I think I was suffering from depression, but I never thought that I was sad. I didn't sleep, I wasn't ever hungry, I felt like my existence had no meaning and I harboured plans of how I would kill myself if I ever did decide to – but I was never *depressed*.

Part of this can probably be explained by placing different ways of understanding depression along a spectrum. At one extreme would be a purely biological view in which the symptoms are objective things such as sleeplessness or lack of appetite. At the other end would be a woollier definition, where the most fundamental symptoms were the illness' effects on my thoughts and feelings. It is mysterious how the two ends of this spectrum could be related to one another. What could something physical, like lack of appetite, have to do with low mood? For me, the problem was an acute one because I did not perceive any low mood at all.

I now think that understanding depression as a purely medical illness can have some negative consequences. In my case, it prevented me from recognising the psychological impact that my situation had upon my mood. By focusing mainly on the objective symptoms, it reinforced my inability to experience my low mood, and so locked me tighter into emptiness. This was not helped by being told that many of the problems I was facing were common for survivors of head injuries. It was all just neurological, apparently, and had nothing to do with what I might be going through or feeling.

Often, I remembered fragments of what I had learnt at school about the philosophy of Descartes, and the difficulty of separating the brain from the mind, and I would muse upon how mysterious it all was. The question that had baffled philosophers for centuries was the same one that my damaged brain had to wrestle with. So I did and this is what I learned.

***

Wednesday 4th August 2010

I've been reading that book that Irina lent me, when I asked her what the meaning of life was. It's by this guy, Viktor Frankl, and he reckons that we all need to find meaning to make our life worth living. I guess that's why I'm so "depressed", because my life doesn't have any meaning. But he says that there's no single 'meaning of life': everyone kind of has their own meaning. That's what keeps us all going.

I guess that's why I never had problems sleeping when I was in hospital, because every day had a kind of meaning: get up, get dressed and go to sessions – always working towards the ultimate goal of getting better. I guess when I got out of hospital, it dawned on me how pointless it was: "that's so last month".

Everyone says how recovery keeps happening until the day you die. OK. I let them tell me I'm not better. Or even that I'm not yet where I will be eventually. But what I find difficult is that no matter how hard I try to will myself to get 'better' it makes no difference in the end.

I guess I just need to find some meaning. So that's my meaning for now: find a point to my existence. Once I have said meaning, then I'll live for whatever that is.

***

Although I told myself that I had no genuine intention of attempting to end my own life, I had thought about it an alarming amount for somebody who was convinced that they were not depressed. (Or to use the correct medical terminology I was experiencing 'suicidal ideation'.)

I would recall a conversation that I had with Najma, when she was suffering from depression, about her difficulties with the word suicide. She said it reminded her that there was a time when it was illegal, and explained how she much preferred to say that someone had "died from depression".

When reflecting upon this I began to harbour a severe dislike of this euphemistic terminology. I felt that if I chose to take my own life, it would be trying to regain control of my existence. It would be a two fingers up to the white society that did not want me to lead a meaningful life, that managed to have some influence on the world around me. They had tried to stop me becoming someone, trying to convince me I had a "head injury", so suicide would be exerting control over what little I could: my death. I had even constructed a suicide note which read "I did not die of depression. I have <u>chosen</u> to end my own life." This was never written down, though: I would never have been foolish enough to let it take a physical form. If anyone knew of my intention to commit suicide, it would make it even harder for me to have a successful attempt.

When thinking about how I would commit suicide, I knew I would find it especially hard because of my cognitive impairments. I would often joke (to myself) that "I wouldn't have the executive functioning needed for a successful attempt." (I was suffering from impaired executive functioning and had difficulties problem solving and remaining outcome-oriented, both of which were somewhat essential for a successful suicide attempt!)

The nearest I came to a plan was deciding that I would Google "how to tie a noose" and hang myself from a hook in the ceiling. The only reason I knew that tying a noose was not a straightforward task was from reading Sylvia Plath's *The Bell Jar* (which I had read as a teenager). I remember a passage in it, where she talks about her embarrassing attempts to hang herself, being unable to tie a noose.

In our house there is a hook attached to the ceiling above the staircase, which I imagined I could exploit for this purpose. However, it was nearly a year later that my executive functioning had improved so that I was able to see the flaw in that plan: there was no way that a hook screwed into a wooden beam would hold my weight. This led me to refine the plan – wait until the DVLA reinstated my driver's licence and use it to hire a car. I would then attach the hose from our hoover to the exhaust (using some of Ben's heavy duty silver duct tape), place one of the heavy stones from our garden on the accelerator. I'd finish this off with putting the tube through the back window to suffocate myself and lie down on the back seat.

***

Tuesday 12th October 2010

... I had an appointment with Dr. Henderson-Slater today. When I was in reception waiting for the taxi back, I was listening to my iPod. Radiohead's The Pyramid Song[114] came on. It really made me think it was a joke that I delude myself that "I was suicidal".

How can I really claim to have been contemplating ending it all, when I haven't even thought about what "the end" means for more than five minutes? Simple answer: I wasn't properly suicidal. People often say that someone hasn't thought about their own death deeply enough before making that choice.

And I guess I hadn't ever really thought what would happen to "me", my soul, whatever. I did know, in the abstract, that I'd go to Hell, but I didn't really know what that means. And I thought it was a small price to pay: my eternity compared with everyone else's present life. But now I think about it, how could a living person ever know what happens?

***

---

[114] Radiohead's *The Pyramid Song* explores what happens to someone after death. It uses the ancient Egyptian idea of the pyramid, in which a person's body is buried with items that they can take with them into the afterlife, to explore what happens to the spirit after death.

Even though I had planned to suffocate myself with car exhaust fumes, I never tainted my laptop's internet history with Google searches for 'car hire company oxford' because this could alert people to my intentions, which were only idle at this stage. I would not be able to teach myself how to clear my browser's history, without asking Ben, which would somewhat defeat the purpose. (The 'old Faiza' never looked at internet pornography, so never learned how to clear the internet history.)

Having to wait for my driver's licence to arrive would also force me to wait, but not postpone the decision indefinitely. A big fear of mine was that I would forget[115] that I wanted to kill myself, but still continue to sap oxygen from this Earth. If I was successful, then it would be the single most important decision of my life, and I should sit on it for at least a few months.

I do, however, think that these thoughts were only idle. I don't think I ever had any real plans to act on them. But, I do have to be reminded that I did have these thoughts whenever I start to think "I didn't really have depression". It also needs pointing out that I only dare to write this now, three years after I crashed the car and a year after managing to pass my driving test, because I have chosen to live, having built a meaningful life for myself.

By the time I had passed my driving test I had <u>chosen</u> to live. Well, for the time being, at least.

---

[115] The word "forget" does not capture why I would not remain outcome orientated, but there is no single word to capture why I might not be able to remain focussed on the original aim.

15 My New Brain

This car crash gave me a new brain. It behaved quite strangely and had a mind of its own. Now I had the wonderful opportunity to start all over again because, we all know how much I enjoyed the experience first time round. But, this time I would make sure I did it well.

Back when I was in the OCE I was supported, even encouraged, to go for visits home. Every week I was given what I called 'weekend leave'. I was told that this would help the process of settling back into normal life. I would always get annoyed when they talked about this long process of gradual adjustment. "Surely you just get released? Why do they have to make a big deal out of everything?"

Ben had to buy a new car to replace the Toyota that I had written off. He bought a large 5 door ultra-safe family machine, motivated by a need for safety. It was in this that he would take me back to the home I couldn't remember. His new safety-conscious heart, however, didn't stay on the scene for long and a few months later he surrendered to his manly desire for a roaring engine, and bought a BMW 3 series (he tells me it had the power of four and a half Yarises). But he would drive me back to the OCE early in the morning in his 'safe' car.

He would force me to emerge from our bed at 07:30 and drop me off on his way to work. I would stay in my pyjamas and get into my hospital bed once there. Then, he would race off to his office in Shepherd's Bush.

As I sat in the passenger seat my mind would wander and I would feel a compulsion to open the door as we zoomed down the outside lane of the A34 at 80 mph. After a few trips catching myself thinking like this this, I did not know what to make of it. "Maybe this is the disinhibited thing they're always talking about." I came to the conclusion that now I was disabled, it stood to reason that I should want to kill myself. I knew that talk of slaughtering disabled people was not socially acceptable, and before the car crash I would never have entertained such an abhorrent idea. "Then it was a disabled person in the abstract, but this is me here and now." Suicide did seem like quite an extreme desire when I was always being told how well I was doing. "Maybe it's just a vague Freudian option?" I never really believed that I would, but after a few drives like this, I would wake myself up enough to lock the door after I got in, just in case.

A couple of years later, I read that damage to the brain can make some patients compulsively pull on a door handle. This was not because of any sort of subconscious desire to escape; it was caused by damage to the frontal lobes. Deterioration of, or injury to, the brain can affect a patient's ability with understanding language and can result in patients' inability to make a distinction between a door handle as a mechanism to open the door with and an instruction to OPEN. I was not suicidal (yet), but this all seems to have triggered a series of difficult questions: "Why don't I kill myself? Is there any point in living now that I am described as someone who is often a burden on their carers?"

I never thought that I was difficult, but I could never be sure because after all that is part of the condition.

***

Thursday 12 November 2009

It's been quite a traumatic week. Traumatic might be a tad OTT, but it was started off by some tiny little thing that happened at the weekend.

Ben was chatting to his parents about what he wanted for Xmas and he said, quelle surprise, something for his guitar. He said he wanted an amp (and he'd already researched it on the web!), but he said that he wouldn't know if it was right until he played on it. So we went to some guitar den on the Cowley Road. As usual we were cutting it fine, getting there with barely enough time for him to give it a good checking out.

Because we had to leave in a rush I forgot to get my phone. I only remembered just as we were leaving the house and Ben said we didn't have time. "You'll be with me, and I've got my phone." We hit traffic. Not really traffic, just people driving too slow for this boy racer in a crazy hurry. We had to park in a Tesco up the road and walk the last bit. I did my best speed hobbling, but it was still too slow to ensure we'd make it in time. I was berating Ben for not letting me get my mobile. ("More speed, less haste.")

Anyway, I was clearly impeding our race to the shop, so he asked if he could sprint off without me. He said "It's just straight down this road on the left. It's got an electric blue sign above the door and you can see guitars in the window. You can't miss it." I did [miss it], though. [116]

---

[116] Neurological patients' processing of visual information is often affected. The sensory information that the optic nerve transforms into electrical signals is processed by the brain's occipital lobe. Sometimes this can be damaged, resulting in survivors being unable to make

I got to a roundabout and thought "Ben didn't mention a roundabout. I must have missed it." So I did a 180° turn. The plan I concocted in my head was to call Ben's parents the moment I passed a phone box and they'd be able to call his mobile. (And I could get him to phone the payphone.) The only flaw in this plan was that I didn't have any cash on me. And, I couldn't even remember the number to dial if you want to make a reverse call. Oh yeah, and the world's moved on since I was little and there aren't any phone boxes around anymore. I couldn't even remember where the Tesco was where we'd parked the car because of my crap memory. (I discovered that this memory becomes even crapper mid-panic.)

So, I stopped my speed hobbling and crept along, making sure I looked in each shop window really carefully and asked any poor randoms that passed, "Where's the nearest payphone?" No one gave me much time, because I imagine I sounded like I was "wrong in the head", with my speech peaking in its general crappiness from the panic that was pumping through my heart.

In the end [probably five minutes later], I heard Ben shout out my name. He might as well have reached out and shaken me by the shoulders, because I was concentrating so hard on making sure that I looked in each shop window to see if there were any guitars.

But the conclusion I have since made is "NEVER LEAVE THE HOUSE, ESPECIALLY NOT WITHOUT YOUR MOBILE." Ever since then I've been even more glued to these four walls than before and I was just starting to get the confidence to walk up to the church on the way to the fields.

Disempowered is the word that all these professionals use. Yeah, that's what I am. People have always been obsessed with making me independent. That was one of the buzz words at the OCE. I always used to think "independence is a bit overrated." I didn't think I minded being dependent on people.

---

proper sense of the information received from the optic nerve. Their eyes can see, but their brains cannot.

In "to see and not to see", in his The Anthropologist On Mars, Oliver Sacks examines the case of a man, Virgil, who was born blind and who subsequently had his eyes "fixed". But his vision was not like that of someone who is born sighted, because his brain was unable to make sense of the electrical signals it receives.

Virgil's condition was just a little bit more disabling than not noticing a particular shop front despite specifically looking out for it! With me, I was essentially not able to be methodical when scanning my visual field. My brain was unable to translate the electrical impulses it received whilst at the same time worrying about not being able to find the shop.

I could understand why THEY wanted to make people independent, because crips are a burden on the able-bodied. I am a sponge for their resources. What I used to resent was the way they all acted like not being dependent on others was somehow beneficial for the disabled person – they kind of assumed "you wouldn't want to be dependent."

But now I see: I wouldn't want to be dependent on someone, just to live. I'm not independent and it's horrible. I don't so much mind that I'm a leach: it's more that I'm so completely at the mercy of whoever.

Ben might not be the type to take advantage, but he can still make mistakes. He's not in my head, so he can't make perfect decisions in the same way that my undisabled counterpart would.

***

My recollection of this time is quite vague: my brain's ability to form new memories was still affected. I was not the busy woman I used to be. Lethargic and housebound, I was quite the typical Countdown-viewer. The old Faiza never really watched it. Not only did she not have time, (managing her successful, busy life), but she was rubbish at it. The longest word she would make was a 4 or 5. Occassionally, a 6.

Then one day I had it on and I immediately spotted an 8. Next round I got a 7. Every round was like this now. I even got the conundrum sometimes.

I was now good at it! It must be the brain injury. The only sense I have been able to make of it has been that my brain does not rigidly hold onto the letters in their set places. They float about freely and words take shape.

I would rarely get worse than a 7. I could keep up with the dictionary corner!

As my 'functioning' improves, I am getting rubbish again.

***

Back when we lived in our flat in Willesden, I remember being quite disappointed when our "brown" sofa was delivered. It was distinctly orange. Certainly more orange than it had looked in the show room. Everyone reassured me that "it looks fine". But it was orange!

One of the last memories I have of Willesden is of remedying our orange sofa crisis. The living room in our new Oxfordshire house had dark stained fitted wooden cupboards. The décor was a bit too heavy for our (my) taste. But our orange sofas could lift the room out of its stuffy middle-aged tendencies. We could make it look as though we had deliberately chosen orange.

"We'll achieve this through putting up orange artwork," I thought.

But we don't have any orange artwork. So I went to the library and got out a book on how to paint still life, buying on my way back a canvas and a bag of oranges. The old Faiza used them to start painting a collection of oranges. After a morning poring over journal articles for her Masters studies, she would stop for a break and paint some more of her masterpiece. (She was always so full of energy.)

The book explained to the reader how to observe light and dark to give depth to the objects. There's a canvas of some oranges on the dark, heavy, wooden mantelpiece. Rather than a painting of three flat orange circles, it shows a collection of three dimensional fruit. Is there no end to this girl's talents?

Then when I was in rehab, I knew that I enjoyed painting so I asked Ben to bring in my acrylics. For some reason, I had become obsessed with Mondrian. There was something about the stark, bold shapes that appealed to me: "He was such a genius. The way he distils everything down to its geometric basics", is what I would have said if I could articulate why I had become obsessed. But the reason I could not was also the reason I had been captivated by his minimalist style.

In our bedroom hangs my other 'masterpiece'. It is a reworking of one of his compositions. Unfortunately, the tremor in my hand made it impossible for me to achieve the clean, smooth lines that are somewhat essential to his minimalist style.

Nearly a year later when we were in Asturias, I took my sketch book with me and managed to produce a pencil sketch of part of the view from our garden. It is clear that my heart was not in it. Sketching is just something that the old Faiza would have done on a holiday to the countryside. I achieved the same: box ticked.

***

The Football World Cup was played in June 2010. It had been a year since I had been released and I was getting bored at home. I had never been a big fan of the game, but I hoped it could help pass the time.

When the first England match was on, we happened to be going round to Ben's parents, so I was going to watch it there with his family. We all sat in the living room. My crippledom earned me the best seat in the house: directly in front of their brand new high definition TV. I was going to make the most of this.

After about 20 minutes the tension in my temples became unbearable. I shut my eyes.

"Are you alright?"

"Yes, I'm fine." Can't I even watch the football without them forming their judgements?

No, I was not fine. At half time I explained how watching the football was making my head hurt and sat in the kitchen with my eyes shut, listening to the Five Live commentary. My analysis of this at the time was, unsurprisingly, an overly scientific one.

"22 players and one ball. That's 23 variables."

I knew, from my teacher training, that the number of items a person can process in their head could be as low as 5. (Working memory is the "magic number seven plus or minus two"[117].) My new brain would not cope. Listening to the commentary on the radio reduced the number of variables my new brain had to compute.

This was how I learned to adapt to my new brain.

---

[117] Gorenflo, Daniel; McConnell, James (1991). "The Most Frequently Cited Journal Articles and Authors in Introductory Psychology Textbooks". *Teaching of Psychology* 18: 8–12

16 Bushra

By trawling through my old emails, I have learned that we moved out of our Willesden Green flat in North-West London on the 18th of July 2008. I still feel as though I live in London. I think I have some vague memories of moving house, but when I was caught deep in the maze of my paranoid delusions, these memories were so hazy, it felt as though they had been planted in my head – like some kind of alien Bluetooth chip. They were certainly not of the same quality and clarity as the memories I formed and accessed with my old, healthy brain.

When we lived in Willesden, I worked as a physics teacher at a school in Camden. I adored this job, but always felt like a bit of a charlatan. For all my enthusiasm for the subject and devotion to the pupils, I never really understood the science of education. Like most teachers, trial and error had taught me what 'worked' in the classroom. At best I had developed a hunch about what led to a good lesson. But what made it work stayed a mystery for the old Faiza's ravenous mind. *That* brain would only ever be satisfied with black-and-white answers, ideally in the form of clear-cut formulae.

After school one day, the science department was given a talk on forthcoming changes to the science national curriculum by Professor Jonathan Osborne, lecturer in Science Education at King's College, London. After listening to his talk, I was left hungry to explore the exciting world that is secondary school science education. I started to realise that what I knew about science education was pathetically small for someone who wanted to forge a career in teaching physics.

That night I looked on the King's College website and did a search for courses that they offered in science education. I decided to take what I often jokingly referred to as a 'gap year' and study for an MA in science education. I never really had a thirst for travel, so I decided to spend the equivalent money on an MA (working as a supply teacher if we were short of cash that year).

On some evenings I would work as a telephone counsellor on the Muslim Youth Helpline. MYH is a free, national, emotional support service available over the telephone, email and internet. It was set up by Mohommad Sadiq, who was driven to set it up after working for another, more secular youth helpline.

The helpline that he used to work for frowned upon discussion of faith so he could never reassure Muslims who phoned in because they feel that they are judged harshly by Allah by reminding them that Allah is al-Ghafoor (the Forgiving). After seeing the number of young Muslims who called in needing counselling he, along with some of his Muslim friends, set up a helpline that catered especially for the needs of young Muslims. Because it was a Muslim-specific helpline, it was able to directly address any difficulties young Muslims had with their faith.

To work as a telephone counsellor for MYH, I was trained in basic listening and counselling skills. When answering the phone, I was asked to use a pseudonym and I chose the name Bushra.

After my car crash I often found myself haunted by the Faiza who inhabits a parallel universe where the Yaris never crashed and left me with a diffuse axonal injury. Perhaps the animal that ran out in front of me lay sleeping in a field. Or maybe I was just a more competent driver and never crashed the car. But in this parallel universe, a more functional Faiza Siddiqui lives. I am haunted by her so often that I decided to name her: Bushra.

It is somewhat ironic that Bushra was the counsellor for MYH, a non-judgemental peer support service. The Bushra who haunts me now is the most judgmental critic of all my actions. She accompanies me everywhere I go, making her own contributions to all my conversations.

***

The scene is a small living area attached to a kitchen, which has white painted walls and a grey tiled floor. It is clean and tidy with a glass circular table, and a two-seater black leather sofa in front of a small TV.

Faiza is sat with Ben and his parents. They are all dressed casually, in western clothes and muted colours. Bushra, however, wears a red cotton shalwar-kameez.

Faiza and Carol are sitting on the settee with the TV on quietly in the background. David is sitting at the table reading a newspaper and Ben is busy in the kitchen making himself some tea and preparing a small snack.

FAIZA: ... and then I met up with Fred for coffee.

CAROL: Sounds like you've been quite busy then.

BUSHRA: For an unemployed little cripple you certainly have been occupied.

FAIZA: Hmm, yeah. But I still wanna be back at work.

DAVID: Are you getting bored at home?

BUSHRA: *Is she bored? She's BRAIN DAMAGED. She can't even read a magazine article, let alone do something productive.*

FAIZA: Well not so much anymore. I've kind of got used to it.

CAROL: Yeah, it always takes time.

FAIZA: It's not really the boredom.

BUSHRA: *Yeah, you haven't even got the imagination to picture an occupied brain. It's too fucked up to even feel bored.*

CAROL: Hmmm.

FAIZA: It's more that I feel like my life's a bit of a waste of space: just sitting at home.

BUSHRA: *Yeah, and you're painfully aware that you're too brain damaged to even execute a plan to bring your miserable existence to an end.*

CAROL: But you are getting that insurance money.

BUSHRA: *Oooh yeah, the insurance money. What are you complaining about?*

FAIZA: Well, yeah. But that just pays me for just sitting at home being disabled.

CAROL: Of course.

FAIZA: Like, I have skills and talents and they're just going to waste.

CAROL: Hmm, yeah. There is that.

BUSHRA: *See what she's not saying: what skills, what talents? They're all property of the old Faiza. YOU don't have skills. YOU don't possess any talents.*

DAVID: But you can still use your talents.

CAROL: Yeah, you've got such a talent for art.

BUSHRA: *Oh yeah. You can paint pretty little pictures. That'll protect the public from your miserable existence. Painting. That's good, keeps you out of white society's way.*

FAIZA: Hmm.

CAROL: *And your mosaicing. I wish I could do stuff like that.*

BUSHRA: *Cementing bits of tile to something else. You certainly are talented!*

FAIZA: Yeah, but I used to do that in my spare time: after a day's work and on weekends.

DAVID: Have you thought about tutoring, one-to-one?

BUSHRA: *Yeah, one on one. That's all you're good for now.*

BEN: We've talked about this. I don't think it's a good idea.

BUSHRA: *And who knows, you might not even be able to manage that! Why risk it? That'll be such a blow to your self-esteem, wouldn't it? And we wouldn't want to damage poor Faiza's self-esteem would we?*

DAVID: Have you thought about voluntary work?

FAIZA: Yeah, but the trouble is that no one entrusts an unpaid worker with anything meaningful.

BUSHRA: *Especially not a brain damaged little cripple like you.*

CAROL: What's stopping you from enjoying spending the time just relaxing at home?

BUSHRA: *Yeah, why can't you just accept that your life's a waste of space?*

BEN: I'd love to be at home like you.

FAIZA: I know.... I just don't know what to do with myself.

BUSHRA: [sarcastically] *Awww, poor you.*

BEN: I know, it's hard for you isn't it?

BUSHRA: See, he agrees!

FAIZA: No, I know I'm wallowing in self-pity. If we could swap places you could spend all day at home playing the guitar.

BEN: [laughs]

FAIZA: But you wouldn't be able to do your solos because your left hand'd be buggered.

BEN: Yeah, exactly. We don't know how it would affect any of us until we've been there.

FAIZA: I know it looks so nice from where you guys are sitting being paid just to sit at home, but.... oh well... I guess I just have to make the best of this.

***

As the months went on, Bushra's judgemental comments became a regular feature of all my conversations. Eventually, though, she began to feel abandoned, sitting on my shoulder all by herself. So, she asked a friend to join her: White Society Paranoia. He could always read signals into every situation: clear signs that showed how Ben, the doctors and my whole 'care team' had collaborated to fabricate the lie that is my head injury. After all, how else would they stop this dangerously radical teacher from brainwashing the next generation?

Wasn't it a bit too convenient that there weren't any physical signs of this alleged disability? The paranoid delusions and my feelings of isolation fed into one another.

I was often told that it was in the best interests of a disabled person to accept their disability. I always heard about people who adapted the way that they approach life, rather than struggle on and fail. I was given their inspiring stories: people who were always better than me at managing their disabilities.

***

Thursday 16 September 2010

... If I was a "good white girl" I would just accept my "disability" and stop labouring under the illusion that my life has a point now. Everyone seems to say that I should wait before going back to work. "What's wrong with 'my functioning'?" I ask, but no one ever answers

that one. Apparently it's a feature of this head injury that you don't know what's wrong with you. How fucking convenient.

At that party people were asking Ami when I'm going to go back to work. I don't know how to say to them, "It might not look like there's anything wrong with me, but if you were white you'd never say that."

I'm a bit sick of all this. Who's right? A few months ago at Humza's birthday thing Sohail did say about how much brighter I seemed since he last saw me.

That does put the whole white society thing into question. It looks like he was saying the same thing, even though he's brown. I guess it is a bit crazy to think it's just people who are white. Maybe it's only the people who make a success of themselves in the outside world. So Sohail's only "white", because he's a successful doctor and successfully manages to conform to our hegemonic society.

But Hamida Auntie's not "white" and even she said that I've changed. Ami said to me that she said how I do look more "serious" now. But I don't have to be cracking jokes to be a good teacher, do I?

***

I have no idea if my cognitive impairments really were "obvious to everyone", as Ben put it. Perhaps people just did not like to dwell on them. Maybe they hadn't been indoctrinated by white society. Or maybe these cognitive impairments are too "subtle" to be noticed by people who do not observe my functioning on a daily basis, in the way that he does.

Maybe one of the reasons that people observed that I am 'more serious' after my head injury, is because damage to the limbic system can affect emotions (specifically the Dentate Gyrus regulates happiness). Also general damage to the brain can result in a larger proportion of it being occupied for concentrating when in conversation. Less of it can devote itself to expressing emotions such as laughter. (And when laughter does occur, the brain struggles to switch it off once it has started.)

As the months rolled on my 'metacognitive' abilities grew, so I began to have more insight into how my thinking had been affected. Everyone seemed pleased at this 'progress', but I had difficulty seeing exactly how this was a good thing.

***

Sunday 5th December 2010

I'm a bit sick of things always changing. I just want them to be still for a little while. I know everyone changes and "grows", but every few months? If they want me to "accept my disability", then I need to know what it is that I have to accept.

I don't want to get any "better"; the latest thing has been that now I'm starting to see what's wrong with me. I know it's not what people should want, but I was so much happier being blissfully ignorant of all of my impairments. Now I'm starting to see just how many things are wrong with me.

For example, today I was putting two things away: the plate on the drying rack and the mug in the cupboard: one was in my left hand, the other in my right. I got confused! Too many variables: left, right; cupboard, drying rack; plate, mug. I can't be a teacher like this!

I guess white society is right.

***

To give balance to the paranoia that I was experiencing, 'White Society' introduced me to his twin brother, 'How Convenient' (or HC to his friends). The paranoia twins remarked on any coincidence that occurred in my life. White Society's comments were always focussed on how this head injury had been planted by the people who run this country. HC's focus was always much broader than that: he claimed that God himself had masterminded this whole event. (HC did make quite a strong argument: if He's all-powerful surely nothing happens without him 'masterminding' it anyway.)

Whenever I noticed how loving a husband I had, I thought "How convenient". HC was in his element when the nice OTs gave me a comprehension worksheet that was designed for head injury patients to understand their own impairments. It discussed the work of the educational psychologists Piaget and Vygotsky, who I just happened to have written my best essay on during my MA. I couldn't really remember what I wrote, but my old brain had formed complex arguments about their theories.

HC would also, in his spare time, act as a career advisor. He explained to me how God had, almost certainly, planned this head injury. I could be anything in education where I did not need to process information on the spot. Here, an MA in education would be essential. "How convenient. It's almost as though someone had planned it."

I have barely scratched the surface of the deep ravine that is filled with such convenient coincidences, but I assure you that the twins could tell you hundreds if pressed.

17 Personality Changes

Early in March 2010, I lay in bed with some words beating around my head insistently. I was becoming accustomed to sleepless nights and I had started to believe that if I couldn't get myself to sleep, then I might as well get up and do something useful.

There was no point in lying in bed – I did not want to be labelled as lazy. What's more, in bed I would only annoy Ben (and I knew that head cases could be selfish and a burden on their carers). So I went to his study, grabbed some scrap paper and I wrote this down:

I woke up,
It's a blessing:
With the mind of a child,
In the body of an old lady.
Haunted by tales of the
Old me.
Hate her
Seems like a dragon,
But a very clever one.

***

After a brain injury, many survivors experience a change to their 'self-concept'. In common with many others, I was left with the nagging doubt that I was not quite who I used to be. Ami often joked to me how the head injury had given me a personality change and made me more reasonable. (Some survivors are often described as less argumentative and more docile than their previous selves.)

Everyone had their own different opinions about who I was and how I functioned. And to make it worse, the person who they said I had become changed every few weeks, months, or years. I would wish I could judge for myself which opinion was right. But who could I trust to make this judgement? Certainly not myself – they all told me that I couldn't think straight since the car crash.

***

Wednesday 4th August 2010

I knew who I was. I always had such a strong sense of identity. At least I thought I did. I can handle that a head injury can give some people personality changes. Thankfully I haven't had one. Well, that's what gets to me. No one ever admits it, but I am different. At least I think I am. At least I hope I am: she sounds like such a bitch.

I was chatting to Najma on the phone about what I think of the old Faiza. I was complaining about how awful she was. But she stopped me from bitching about her behind her back, saying that she was always quite fond of her. Well, I guess she was her best friend!

But I do think that the old Faiza was a bitch. When Ben tells me stuff that "I" used to say, it does sound quite annoying. I think I was definitely more tense than I am now. Maybe that's how she got all this stuff done, because she was more uptight and her 'functioning' excelled.

Or am I just jealous of her? Kind of like sibling rivalry. I don't think so — she does sound like a genuine bitch.

Tuesday 1st February 2011

It annoys me when people say that I'm no different to who I was before. Ben made me think about how they do it to reassure me, but I think they're just lying to me: I am different. But what do I want to be: old me or new me?

I don't really know what I want them to say.

I think I still feel like me, but I know I'm not clever anymore. Not that I think that's the be-all and end-all. But cleverness isn't just about doing sudokus, it's about stuff that matters too.

I don't think I'm as quick, whatever that means. I have something to say, but can't get it out without seizing up. Or worse still: stop the conversation to say something and then when the floor's cleared for the cripple, I forget what I have to say.

I want to explain, especially if there's someone who didn't know the old me, that I'm not really such a dim wit: I've been in a car crash. But so what? Factually, I am this slow. The car crash is just the reason.

And maybe this is just temporary? Isn't it progress that I realise that I am slow, rather than just thinking I'm no different to before? An OT would praise me! I got better enough to walk, and now better enough to realise what's wrong with me. Maybe it's only a matter of time before the bit of the wit gland gets repaired.

***

As I was struggling to understand my disability, I felt that my aunt was living in a world that was oddly parallel. Soon after I was admitted to the OCE, she was diagnosed as having a brain tumour and had to have surgery for its removal. She is suffering from dementia and has had to live in a residential care home since. She seemed to be isolated in a world where nothing made sense. I know, I had been there, but she was going in deeper and deeper, while I was making my escape from this hell.[118]

It was heart-breaking to talk to her. This was only magnified by her affected emotional control. She would definitely be described as 'emotionally labile'. As with most personality changes after brain injury, family can struggle to understand it: they succumb to temptations to explain this away as nothing more than an extension of her previous personality. But, we need to remember that its origin is largely biological.

What you see is emotional incontinence: once an extreme emotion has started, it is hard for it to stop. The emotion is not necessarily felt more acutely as compared to someone without the injury – it is just expressed more extremely. I tended to be overcome by laughter, whereas my aunt tended to cry more frequently and expressively. For some people, the difficulty can be that they are overcome with anger. When I am angry or get the giggles at an inappropriate time, I transfer my consciousness onto reciting the seven-times table. It does not always work, but when it does, it can help me regain my composure.

This is a diary entry I wrote about a visit to her:

---

[118] It probably needs pointing out that dementia and injury to the brain are distinct conditions. Generally speaking, an Acquired Brain Injury causes selective impairments, leaving people with preserved skills, whereas people with dementia tend to be affected more generally as the disease progresses. The symptoms that my aunt had from the brain tumour were more akin to a brain injury. The ones from her dementia, however, presented more globally.

Monday 21ˢᵗ February 2011

Went to see Beeapa [auntie].¹¹⁹ I found it quite nice, despite being prepared for the worst. She did seem a lot "iller" than last time I visited. Was that her being more affected, or was it just me being better? Maybe I could pick up more on the "subtle" presentation of her symptoms?

Perversely I found the whole thing quite interesting: being on the other side of the neurological disorder fence.¹²⁰ She's quite emotionally labile. Once I twigged that (within seconds of seeing her!) she was so much easier to "manage". I felt awful knowing how demoralizing it used to be (is?) for me when I discovered that I had to be "managed" and no one took me seriously.

I think that I always had a sneaking suspicion that something was up, but I just didn't know what to make of it. Having a rubbish brain never helped.

It looks like Beeapa's at that stage now. She's kind of like I was after I'd been in the OCE for a bit: knows something's up, but not because of any personal insight, just because of the way people act around her.

I remember when I said to Suzy [my psychologist] about how I couldn't rely on my own personal view of things because I was so brain-damaged. But she just said, "I think that you're a patient who has a great deal of personal insight." Always with her condescending little tone of "Yeah, for a head case."

I just wanted to yell back, "It's not really insight: it's just all this stuff I've heard about the way that people with head injuries behave." All that stuff that Ben read me off the internet. It was never ME who had this "insight". I think her 'personal insight yardstick' was a bit skewed anyway: spending all of her professional life interacting almost exclusively with other head cases. So, I couldn't really trust a word she said.

It does annoy me when the "elders" put all of Beeapa's teariness down to Sunna Baji [my aunt's daughter] for "dumping her in a home, when she's perfectly healthy." Physically, yeah! They just don't have a clue.

---

¹¹⁹ 'Beeapa' is a diminutive of 'sister' (apa) and is how my mother would refer to my aunt (or my khala).

¹²⁰ John Bayley's memoir, *Iris*, explores the experience of caring for someone suffering from a neurological condition with much more insight than I ever could. His book gives a loving and honest account of his experience of caring for his wife, who was suffering from Alzheimer's.

That's the only kind of health that's on these people's radar. They never quite get what's wrong with me, why I won't go back to work. I can just see them thinking, "she never used to be lazy, but I guess you never can tell." Their understanding isn't even advanced enough to think, "Maybe it's the head injury that's made her lazy". [121]

Beeapa periodically asks when she's going to come out of hospital. And I feel wrong doing what everyone else does, saying "soon inshAllah" and hoping that she'll forget.

Kind of like I did, she doesn't have a sense of time passing. So she won't be able to compute when months or years have passed by and she's still there and this elusive "soon" still hasn't arrived. Is it wrong? No: it's "for the best".

She also talks about suicide periodically and asks me to pray to Allah for her death. It's horrible, but I don't blame her. I thought of saying something that had once applied to me, but I wasn't callous enough to actually say it: "Yeah, that's understandable, but you don't really have the cognitive functioning needed to plan and execute the involved task of taking your own life."

I think I do understand, though. I feel quite strongly about all of this, and fought my desire to cave into the pressure to just say, "No, don't talk like that, that's not what we want."

I mean, why does it matter what WE want? It's her life that she's thinking about ending. I don't have the right to push my easily-bought optimism onto her. She might not have to live in physical pain, but she's certainly not happy and that's something we have to respect. So instead I said "It's not up to us: it's Allah's choice when we're taken."

Sometimes, when she asked me when she's getting out of this hospital, I just said that I didn't know and she should work on making herself happy here, suggesting that she find little activities to keep herself busy. So she mocked me and said that I should join the nurses in her home. It struck me - I've become what I hate: one of the establishment with their 'helpful' little suggestions.

Anyway, this diary is meant to record my achievements, so here's one... I made it on the train to Manchester by myself. Granted: Ben sat me on the train in Oxford and Omar Bhai picked me up from the station in Manchester. But I made it from the platform to the station reception unaided. Even showed my ticket to the man!

---

[121] Head injury victims are often described as lazy by those around them. This is normally because of the role the brain plays in controlling both the mental and physical energy levels and its subject. These are mediated through the control it has over the production of a variety of hormones, such as serotonin and luteinizing hormone. Often brain injury victims can be overcome with fatigue. When coupled with cognitive problems to memory, organisation ability and initiative, people can often see the victim as 'lazy'.

But that was after spending the whole train journey painfully aware I was way out of my comfort zone, panicking every time we went round a hill and my phone lost signal. I don't really know what danger was bearing down on me, but that didn't stop me worrying.

So now, next time I worry I can say, "I panicked all the way to Manchester and nothing happened to me, so as long as I panic this time too, I should make it there fine."

I'm a stone's throw away from panicking just to be on the safe side. Maybe I should start panicking about getting some kind of anxiety disorder? But the old Faiza would never panic, and this head injury's made me chill out, hasn't it?

***

Of course it affected me to hear Beeapa talk about her own death so frequently and with such lability. It would be heartless if I did not take a moment to pass comment on it. It was horrible to hear. It was certainly more horrible for her to live with the reality of these thoughts in every moment: constantly reliving it because of her memory problems.

There is no escaping the fact that this was horrible. For everyone.

18 Euthanasia

The scene is a domestic kitchen decorated in a traditional style with wooden cupboards filled with clutter. It is a busy kitchen where people are assembled around a round central table, helping to clear up after lunch. Everyone is occupied, chatting and carrying out small domestic chores: loading the dishwasher, making tea or putting away leftovers.

They are all dressed casually.

FAIZA: I can't do that weekend. I'm going to visit my aunt.

CAROL: Oh – which one?

FAIZA: Beeapa. You know, my Mum's sister.

CAROL: The Manchester one?

FAIZA: Yeah. Yeah.

CAROL: How is she now?

FAIZA: Physically, she's doing really well. But she's not very happy. It's hard to explain.

GRANDAD: 'Cause she's in a home, isn't she?

CAROL: And she's not happy there, is she?

GRANDAD: But who's happy when they've been put in a home?

FAIZA: I don't think homes have to be bad.

GRANDAD: No?

FAIZA: They just get a bad press. It doesn't <u>have</u> to be miserable.

CAROL: Hmm.

FAIZA: Obviously I don't know, but I don't think I'd mind being in one.

CAROL: Oh God I would: the décor.

BEN: Well, not just the décor. Things like not being able to get yourself to the toilet.

GRANDAD: Having a catheter in.

FAIZA: And not just for number ones.

GRANDAD: Book a ticket to Geneva when that happens to me.

[All laugh]

FAIZA: I still don't think homes are that bad.

CAROL: No?

FAIZA: I quite liked it when I was in the OCE.

CAROL: But that was quite different.

FAIZA: I know, but you just have to make yourself happy there and kind of accept it.

CAROL: I don't know if we all can do that.

FAIZA: Yeah, it's not easy. But I think that's kind of what you have to do.

CAROL: Mmm.

FAIZA: I think the people who can accept it end up happier.

BEN: But you were quite different.

FAIZA: Yeah, I know – I had lots to do and people came to visit.

BEN: Not just then. But, when you couldn't control your bowel...

FAIZA: Yeah, I know, I was too out of it to know what was going on.

CAROL: Yeah, that was an awful time.

FAIZA: Well, yeah, but the mentality you have makes such a difference.

BEN: And we all made sure we put quite a good spin on it.

CAROL: I think Ben told us all how to talk about it.

NANNY: Yeah, he managed us all and gave us a bit of a briefing!

FAIZA: But about euthanasia... we don't get to choose when we go, do we? And I think that's kind of a good thing.

CAROL: Well, I wouldn't want to be a burden on anyone.

FAIZA: Well, no. But, Carol, you wouldn't be a burden. I mean you gave life to Ben. The least he could do is put up with you in your dying days.

BEN: [laughing] Steady on.

FAIZA: No, I'm serious. I'm not saying you should nurse her and mop up her poos. But have her put down?!

BEN: What – if you're in mind-numbing pain?

FAIZA: Well, OK, maybe in some exceptional circumstances. But I just think people talk about the whole idea quite glibly.

BEN: That's true. I guess we don't really mean it <u>then</u>.

FAIZA: We can all put up with quite crappy lives if we don't have a choice. I mean, I lived with quite a crap body.

[Ben opens mouth to say something.]

FAIZA: Yeah, I know it was different for me because I got *better*, but still, in that moment we didn't *know* that it would turn out OK in the end. Does the trajectory make that much difference to how much the illness matters?

BEN: Yes, of course it does. So many more resources got spent on you and...

FAIZA: And I guess they could teach me stuff knowing that I'll get better.

BEN: And you did, but we didn't know that you would.

FAIZA: But the point still stands.

BEN: Hmm?

FAIZA: If you poo yourself it's gross in that moment – does it matter if you're going to poo yourself less or if you poo yourself just as often until you die? I mean, it's only poo.

BEN: But it's more than just poo... It's general indignity.

FAIZA: Well, you know how I think that dignity's over-rated.

CAROL: I think Ben means things like losing your mind.

BEN: Yeah.

FAIZA: Because people might reveal stuff about themselves, like sides of their personality that they wanna keep under wraps?

BEN: Just behaving in ways that you wouldn't have wanted.

FAIZA: I guess so. But if we legalise it, I know that people will feel under pressure to have it done.

GRANDAD: Of course they would.

FAIZA: I know I would. I think we should just accept the cards that Allah deals us.

CAROL: What if you don't believe in God?

19 Memory

Memory defines who we are. With no continuous sense of ourselves through time, what makes us human starts to break down.

In Proust's *À la Recherche du Temps Perdu* the unnamed narrator tastes a madeleine cake and the smell transports him back to his childhood memory of this taste. A whole world of sensations and meanings is opened up for him. His story is told in a novel, where Marcel Proust examines the nature of memory. His writing was cut short by his death in 1922 and his work was left unfinished, after seven long volumes. If nothing else, it shows us that memory is complicated.

My memory was part of who I was. My new memory is becoming part of who I am now.

Before my head injury I had an excellent memory. While chatting with school friends my overly retentive memory was the butt of many jokes.

"Remember, we did it in geography with Mrs Wood."

"Yeah, but no one remembers it now. Apart from you."

It is somewhat ironic that now I have memory problems. Maybe I am getting my just desserts for my arrogance in the PBI (pre-brain injury) era.

I have learnt that memory is a complicated beast: it has four levels. The first is sensory memory (SM), which we would not normally think of as memory. SM retains only impressions of sensory information after the original stimulus has ceased. A good example is the shapes we make from a sparkler.

On the next level there is working memory (WM). WM is short lived with a limited capacity: it lasts for only a few minutes and is limited to 7 ± 2. My WM was (and still is) affected. My mental arithmetic was appalling. At first, Ben tells me, I could do $3 + 4 = 7$, but $7 + 4 = 11$ was too hard because I could not hold the numbers in my head – I would need to go from single digits to a double-digit number. It was too much to ask my WM to hold one ten in my head, while I added up the remaining units.

The last two types of memory, implicit and explicit, focus on the longer term. Implicit memories are mainly made up of procedural memories: the things we do automatically, things like riding a bike or driving a car. (It turns out that it is possible to forget how to ride a bike, as it is possible to lose an implicit memory.) This includes what physiotherapists call 'muscle memory[122]', but there is much more to procedural memory than control of the muscles.

Explicit memory is the conscious, intentional recollection of an implicit memory. It is made up of semantic and episodic memories. Semantic memory refers to the recollection of concept-based memories and episodic memory deals with recall of the specific details of an autobiographical event.

After my head injury, people's laziness of thought was the bane of my existence. They frequently talked about 'memory problems' as though that encapsulated all of the diverse cognitive effects of my head injury. While it was true that I did have memory problems, it was lazy because it never mentioned what exactly I had forgotten, or the wider problems with thinking which depend on memory.

When I was in the John Radcliffe and a nurse came to take my weight, I told her that, really, she wanted to measure my mass. I treated her to a lecture on the difference between the amount of matter in a body (mass) and the gravitational attraction between that body and the mass of the Earth (weight). My long-term, semantic memory had been unaffected; evidently my social judgement about appropriate conversation had been.

Then, when Ben arrived, I said to him conspiratorially, "Shh! My parents will be here in a bit." I was frightened that my mum would see us together: trapped in a time when I was still living with my parents in Harrow, seeing Ben in secret on holidays from University. I did not want to be caught out and seen with a white boy.

***

People who have suffered head injuries, we were told at CRG, not only forget things, but can also have 'fictitious memories'. Sufferers, we were taught, can invent facts to fill in the blanks in their damaged brains and need to proceed with caution when drawing conclusions from memory of such an event. Without

---

[122] Muscle memory can also be called "motor programming". If you want to pick something off a table you just do it. No one thinks "I need to extend my arm, open hand...", because these pathways are formed in childhood. This is why children do repeated movements of the same thing, such as posting shapes in a toy letterbox- they are forming the motor programmes in their head so that they can do it without thinking later in life.

intentionally lying, then, the survivor can act on memories based on a fictitious event.

"Thank God. I've never had that," I thought. "I'd be really screwed then."

But I am confident with my memory of this event: the few weeks between getting A-level results and starting university, packing for the unknown life ahead took over. Not many of our family friends had lived away from home when at university, but there was someone I could ask about what to buy. Noreen was a bit of a 'rebel' (she did a degree in English literature and lived in halls of residence for University). She told me that a dressing gown is an absolute essential for a woman wanting to maintain her modesty (and body heat) for when the fire alarm goes off in the middle of the night. This sounded sensible, so I when out with a friend and saw a "Little Miss Naughty" dressing gown for sale on in La Senza, I bought it and hung it on the door of L15 (my first year college room).

Ben brought this dressing gown into hospital for me, and it hung on the back of the door there too. "That looks really snug," the OT said to me when getting out of the shower in an OT 'wash & dress' session, "What does it say on it?"

I told her how Ben bought it as a present for me while we were at university. "I know it's meant to be kinky," I said, "But he just bought it for me because I never do as I'm told." This fitted in quite well with the narrative I had of our relationship. But I wasn't telling the truth. However, my lip did not curl up in the way that it does when I'm lying.

***

Textbooks describe anterograde amnesia as the inability to form new memories. But underlying every textbook case is an actual person. The most famous case of anterograde amnesia was Henry Gustav Molaison, born in the 1920s. He is now known as HM, the famous American memory disorder patient. He had had epilepsy from a young age, which was put down to a head injury he could have incurred falling off his bicycle when he was aged eight. He suffered from tonic-clonic seizures and he was referred to William Beecher Scoville for treatment in 1953.

Scoville localized HM's epilepsy to his medial temporal lobes and suggested their surgical removal as a treatment. On September 1, 1953, Scoville removed parts of HM's medial temporal lobes on both sides of his brain and approximately two-thirds of HM's hippocampus was taken from him. The surgery was successful: HM's distressing epileptic fits were cured, and he should have been able to fit back into normal society.

But he was not normal. He now suffered from severe anterograde amnesia: he could not commit new events to long-term memory. He had also suffered moderate retrograde amnesia, and could not remember most of the 1-2 year period before surgery.

Then, in 1962 Suzanne Corkin worked with him. She spent countless hours testing him and talking to him. She knew intimate details about his life, but to him she always remained a stranger: he could never remember who she was.

In their sessions together she would often ask him to trace a five pointed star from its reflection in a mirror. Every time HM sat down to do this he was convinced it was the first time he had done it. But each time he did it, he was faster than the last. So, even though he had no recollection of doing it, he managed to acquire a new skill. The same man, who could not form any long term memories, learnt something new.

This was ground-breaking: a tiny area in the middle of the brain supports memory, but not ALL types of memory.

***

As well as anterograde amnesia, I am told that I had retrograde amnesia. For me, this meant that I had lost access to memories made in the couple of years before the car crash. At its worst this included memories I had made of Ben: I am told that I could not recognise him. I still cannot remember moving to Oxford, but have come to accept it. I have heard many stories and seen lots of pictures, but I still can't remember it. At least, I think I can't.

Freud calls the sort of memories I have of this time 'screen memories'. Screen memories are events that you have been told about, and reconstructed from other people's recollections, letters, photographs and videos as if you had experienced them yourself. But they are not based on the personal impressions that you had at that time.

My new brain is rubbish at forming its own new memories.

***

Monday 7 February 2011

I just had a really life-changing experience. Or rather, the new Faiza had a seminal moment. We were driving down some back road in Willesden Green[123] on the way to Alex and Nicki's. And we took some little back road and Ben was saying that it's round the other side of Gladstone Park and it comes out further up along the A5. And he was describing the path the road takes, delighting in the fact that we know all these obscure back roads in our little patch of North-West London. And I was so happy because I forgot something... and it felt like when I forgot something in the old days!

Hurrah. The old Faiza's back.

It kind of frustrates me when people say "we all forget stuff", mistakenly thinking that it's going to somehow going to reassure me. It always leaves me feeling that I was making a big deal out of something everyone experiences. I just make a fuss out of it whereas they get on with it. I always kind of felt that the forgetting that they talked about was in some way different, but I could never express how. Now I KNOW it is different because I've just had a normal forgetting moment and it was SO different.

The brain damage memory loss feels like you're going down a road and then it suddenly turns blank: you're walking along, you come to a road and out of nowhere there's nothing but a giant blank with just a big sign saying "Situation vacant: insert memory here."

But then this forgetting felt like the normal memory loss of old times. It felt like walking down a road and then it becomes all foggy and you can't really make things out properly.

I hate to say it, but the annoying OT lingo did hit the nail on the head: the memories now are "patchy", whereas before forgetting stuff just made stuff hazy.

***

My consultant from when I was an in-patient, Professor Udo Kischka, came to talk to the cognitive rehabilitation group I attended at the OCE. We head cases attending it had a massive number of questions about the biology of brain damage. Understandably, the psychologists and OTs felt out of their depth answering involved medical questions about neurobiology. They all had a lot of experience with head injuries, but none of them were medical doctors.

He used his medical knowledge to explain to us that the key to recovery is learning ways to adapt to the able-bodied world that we live in and not living in the

---

[123] Willesden Green is the area in London where we used to live before moving to Oxford.

hope that someone will just wave a magic wand and make it all better. (Of course the able bodied world should also adapt to be made to be more accessible.) I suspect this is what motivated him to say what he did.

He told us that once a brain cell had died, it could not come back to life. None of us liked to hear it, because surely there's a chance of the old me coming back? No, you've been told by a professor of neuroscience: once they're dead, they're dead.

I put up my hand and asked "How can you say that? My memory has definitely got better since I was in here."

He told me that concentration and the ability to form memories had probably got better. Apart from the brain bruising that heals in the first few months, there is no further recovery. Factually, the neurones that died remain dead.

It is only two years after that that I had developed the cognitive ability to research this for myself. I learned how neurogenesis can occur in the hippocampus (the area of the brain where memories are made).[124] Professor Kischka most likely didn't mention this, because he was trying to emphasise the need for us to accept our disabilities. And his judgement probably told him that it was not a wise move to enter into an involved discourse on neurogenesis with a room full of brain-damaged crips who, for the last year, had been told that tying their own shoe laces was a tremendous achievement. We probably weren't the best audience.

***

Sometime during my last month at the OCE, I remember having a flashback. To tell you the truth, I can't actually remember having the dream, but I do remember walking out the garden, that afternoon, and talking to someone who seemed to recognise me. Rachel was visiting the OCE for a meeting and told me she used to be my physio when I was in the JR. She told me, something that irritated me: that she was really pleased to see how far I had come on. We chatted about how I know that, factually, I had been in the JR, but I don't remember it. Then I told her how last night I had a dream and wondered if this might the sort of thing they call a flashback. She said that it sounds like it could be was a "flashback" of my time on the neurosciences ward at the JR.

So, this is it...

---

[124] G. Neves, G; S.F. Cooke and T.V. Bliss (2008). "Synaptic plasticity, memory and the hippocampus: A neural network approach to causality". Nature Reviews Neuroscience 9 (1): 65–75.

I was in hospital, but I was also sitting in economy class on a PIA (Pakistani International Airlines) flight. The legroom was non-existent and I couldn't move my legs because, as usual, we had such an excessive quantity of hand-baggage: a holdall was squeezed into the gap between me and the seat in front.

That is all that I remember of the months of my coma.

20 Recovering

Tuesday 8ᵗʰ December 2009

I had an appointment with Jane from the OCE today. She came round and we talked through what we could do together. I'm really pleased with how it all went. She said something about some experimental new programme they had for developing "upper limb functionality".

They seem to be quite forward thinking about head injury rehab (like this experimental new upper limb stuff). And I guess she does know me from when I was in the OCE.

We talked a bit about voluntary work too. She seemed to be quite up for it. It never came up with the other lot. I heavily suspect they would have just said, "You? Voluntary work?! What will it take for you to realise that you've had a head injury?" It did come up when was I was going to be working with other head cases and they seemed to act like that was already me biting off more than I could chew. Of course they were very careful not to say anything discouraging out loud.

And then she told me about the next thing they had in store for me. She had a little worksheet about our next task. It was all quite well presented. Not only in that it had been word-processed. It was presented as "a challenge", even though they knew it was in no way going to be challenging for me.[125]

Rather than say "We want to see you on a bus to see how well you can cope with independent travel", she gave me a sheet outlining my "challenge". I have to get there by bus, meet Hannah at this place called "the Carfax tower" in the centre of Oxford, then "complete two tasks of my own choosing". Then I get to have a coffee with Hannah.

They've left it up to me to pick my own tasks, in my own time, print off a route and google the right shops. They don't feel it's necessary to sit with me, holding my hand, while I sit on the PC looking up bookshops in Oxford.

***

---

125 It is important with head injuries to set an achievable task for the patient. It is also important that the patient does not find the task a patronising demand.

Ben pointed out to me that because they had a sense of the rate of neurological recovery, they visited less frequently than the other OTs. So they only talked to me about my next task over a month later. They also worked on my physical functioning: the task's aim was to improve my impaired upper limb functioning (or "make my crap hand better").

Jane or Hannah, I forget who, explained what I would need to do for the 'constraint induced motion therapy'. After reading the introduction to the literature that they gave me, I learnt about how it had shown massive improvements for other patients. It explained that it's best when the patient uses CIMT to perform functional tasks that they need to do anyway.

Ever since the 'new Faiza' had moved to our house in Oxford, I felt that it lacked a woman's touch. I would love to excuse Ben's lack of hygiene by the stress of having to care for his disabled wife, but Ben has never, to put it lightly, been at all house-proud. So, this seemed like an ideal opportunity to put my clean and tidy stamp on it. This stamp wore off within a week and we have never really managed to re-establish it.

***

Thursday 11th March 2010

Jane came round with some gumph on this thing called CIMT. It's the "experimental new technique" that I was so excited about. They tie up your good hand with a bandage and so you're forced to use your impaired limb to do everything. I'm quite disappointed: the only thing "experimental" about it is the number of hours you do it for. I thought there'd at least be some special bandage.

Anyway, I asked her if I'd come into the OCE and they'd train up my hand there, but she just said that I do stuff around the house myself. She said that I should make a little timetable for myself and use it to discipline myself. But I'm quite a disciplined person anyway.

And she says there are two ways to do it: a short sharp blow, or a bit more gentle thing stretched over months. I think I want the short sharp blow. It's not like I think there's loads wrong with my hand anyway. I'm OK with a slightly shitty hand, but I just want to be told that I'm better NOW. And if this is one of the stupid hoops I need to jump through to get that: then bring it on.

They do give you weekends off though. That's part of the deal. I'm not a wuss, though — I probably won't need them. But that's the deal with this "experimental new technique". I HAVE to rest.

I was thinking I might use this time to get the house back in order. It really went to rack and ruin when I was in hospital. I cleaned it up for my "coming out party", but it's disintegrated again. Not quite as bad as it was back then, but it's still not clean. So, I'm going to use this CIMT time to rein it in.

***

"Bring it on" became the attitude that saw me through this time. Without it I'd still be a little cripple whinging to herself about how life has been so hard on her. No matter how able bodied we might be, don't we all need to embrace the shit that life throws at us?

The "shit" that I needed to embrace now, was 6 hours a day for 2 weeks of this CIMT. During the activities healthy, undamaged neurones forged new paths to avoid the damaged cells. Jane advised me to make a timetable of functional tasks that I could do around the house to help motivate and pace myself. (I know it was Jane, because she sent me an email with this advice.) She advised me not to plan too much for one session and to ensure that I place breaks at regular intervals. This would help to prevent fatigue. The treatment literature stipulated that I would need the weekends off for recuperation. I did not think I would need them, because "I'm a motivated and driven person." But at the weekends I would be exhausted and would do little more than sleep, eat and listen to radio 4, all the while rejoicing in the bi-manual glory of my unconstrained limbs.

I did begin to notice improvements after just a few days. Here is an email that I wrote with my left hand:

To: Najma Warsi
Date: Wed 14/04/2010 18:20

I've been to the GP re counselling and he told me to come back once he's had a chance to talk to the OCE. He sent me off with one of those questionnaires, when they ask you questions like "do you have difficulty sleeping? 1. not at all... 4. every night" the questionnaire was useless like I thought it would be, a lot of the symptoms of depression overlap with brain damage ones e.g. concentration, trouble sleeping. We'll see what he says. At my last session with the psychologist she said that the GP contacted her with reference to my desire to see a counsellor and she said that if I see a counsellor then I can't see her at the same time and so I'm not complaining.

I'm having the constraint induced therapy at the mo'. This is my 2nd day. But I've already noticed a few changes. Yesterday after I'd taken the bandage off I completely spontaneously picked up a chip when eating my dinner. It made me realise that it's really psychological. By psychological I don't really mean "believing that you have enough strength to pick up a 10g finger sized cuboid with your affected limb", I mean more neuro-psychologically (forming the pathways in your brain etc.)

F

xx

***

After a day's CIMT I would be swallowed up by 'fatigue'. Ben would come home after work to find me abnormally emotional. Although since my head injury I have never been able to actually cry, I would meet him at the door telling him just how much I love him. He might then respond with a light hearted comment, to which I would laugh uncontrollably. It would then strike me just how much of a head injury cliché I was being, triggering yet more laughter. I would then be overcome with shame at how this is not the same woman that poor Ben fell in love with all those years ago. Eventually, he would advise me to go to bed. I would reluctantly agree, knowing that I would be unable to sleep.

Then the next morning my alarm would go off for me to start another day of this therapy.

***

Monday 19th April 2010

I spent the last couple of weeks doing my CIMT. I had the weekends off, but had to spend most of them sleeping and lying in bed. It's been really knackering and I'm not sure it was worth it. I stupidly never thought it would be so tiring, but I guess it makes sense when you think about it.

I told Naveed about thinking "was it worth it: the improvement to my hand has been barely noticeable, but I became incredibly silly with all the tiredness." But then he said "but this is the hand you'll have for the rest of your life."

Tuesday 10th May 2011

That CIMT really did work. Just small things, but I can definitely do more stuff with that hand now compared with X amount of time ago. The actual training I gave my hand started me on an upward spiral. I started using my hand more (albeit crapply, at first), so more synaptic connections would form and I would use it for more and more fiddly stuff.

Was it worth it? Yes. Does that mean I would I do it again to get some more improvements? No, because I'm quite happy with my "upper limb functioning", now.

This is the question with everything: if I'm happy with who I am now, then what does that say about the impaired Faiza who was here 6 months ago? And how dissatisfied will the Faiza of a year's time be with this Faiza here today?

21 On The Road

A month after discharge I had an appointment with Professor Kischka. He seemed really pleased with my progress and I remember him saying, in his positive and encouraging manner, how he thought that I should be able to return to driving one day. In response I smiled and said, "That's good to hear." But I did sit there thinking, "I didn't even know there was a chance I wouldn't be able to!" It dawned on me that there must be more to head injuries than I thought.

Then that winter it snowed, and Ben's new fancy BMW (which he had bought in a post-accident, euphoric, seize-the-day spending splurge) got stuck in it. As he could not push and steer at the same time, I sat behind the wheel while Ben pushed it free, all the time joking about how naughty we were being because the DVLA still had my licence. "What if they caught me behind the wheel in this knob-wagon? They'd never let me drive then." Luckily, though, they never did catch us breaking the law.

Most people that I spoke to thought I would have to overcome a fear of driving. But this was not my problem. In fact, nervousness was one of the smallest hurdles I had to overcome, since I had no memory of the actual crash. In fact, it was quite the opposite because I had an impaired judgment of risk. I was over-confident and was oblivious to the fact that I was driving like a nutter.

When I was an in-patient I had seen posters in the OCE explaining that after a head injury, you are required to inform the DVLA. I knew that after an epileptic fit the DVLA suspended your licence and I saw this stipulation as an unnecessary medical rule to which one had to conform. I could not appreciate the full reasoning behind this until just a few weeks before successfully passing my test.

A few months later I had an assessment with RDAC (the regional driving assessment centre). I felt that my driving was a bit worse than normal, but I just put this down to the fact that I hadn't driven for over a year. The assessor accepted that the long break might be able to partly explain it, but he maintained it was unlikely to be just that.

I have now come to understand that my lack of understanding was not unusual. People only tend to understand physical impairments. Even driving instructors themselves have a poor understanding of the cognitive barriers that some disabled people face. The main reason, which I could not understand at the time, is that following such an injury, the brain cannot process information about the road quickly enough to allow safe control of the car.

Often people would ask me "Can you remember how to drive?" The answer to this question was always "Yes". I know the sound the engine makes when you need to change from first to second gear. I know what the biting point feels like. But, looking back, I can see that although the question managed to capture something about the neurology, it was overwhelmingly crude. It never said much about the actual difficulties that head injury survivors have with relearning to drive, as there is much more to cognitive functioning than just memory problems. Processing hazards and 'reading the road' is what survivors have to conquer.

***

Friday 16th April 2010

Jenny [Paige, my physiotherapist] came round to show me some stretches. She was asking me how driving was going and if I'd had any joy finding an instructor. I said that I might need to go on an automatic and she said I should be able to drive a manual.

I told Ben this and he said that I'd probably need to learn on an automatic because of my processing speed!

But I guess that's alright because it's just changing gears and stuff like that. I mean it's not quantum mechanics...

***

When spring came I had to go on a drive with the DVLA. I was blissfully unaware that this was a formal driving assessment. I saw it as yet another pointless formality, unaware that if I drove well, my licence would be reinstated. Or, that if I drove badly, I would be banned from driving for even longer.

I thought I drove OK. But Ben, who sat in the back, now tells me that I was really bad. After 10 minutes of the assessment, I was given an automatic to drive and I was apparently, "better, but still quite scary."

Then, early that summer my provisional licence arrived in the post with a letter explaining that I should prepare for another assessment in the autumn. So I set about trying to find an instructor. I was not really in the best position to be able to explain my impairments to driving schools. I pleaded with Ben to let me at least try and pass on a manual, all the time insisting that "My left hand isn't so crap that it can't hold a gear stick".

I had my first lesson about one year after the brain injury. Ben was angling for half hour lessons because of my 'fatigue' – a word he often used, having appropriated it from medical websites – but I always felt that this was unfair because I was never tired. I would not *feel* tired, but was always told that my 'functioning' was acutely affected.

It was as though my brain had been switched off right from the inside. Or as I put it, "My head's too exhausted to waste brain calories on telling me that I'm tired": unaware that I was tired because I had no concept of this kind of tiredness to begin with. There seemed to be a whole land inside my skull that I was not aware of, where strange men were flicking switches at random, while I was left feeling the after-effects of what they did.

But we did not have the luxury of a choice between driving instructors and most driving schools seemed flummoxed when we asked about half hour lessons. A few days later an instructor from a well-known driving school arrived with an automatic and we went for a lesson. Again, I felt like my driving was OK, but I did not share that point of view with the man whose vehicle it was. He ended the lesson 15 minutes early, excusing himself claiming he had to "be somewhere". Then when I tried to book the next lesson he told me he would have to refer me to his boss and the driving school directly. They never did call me.

Later that month, Ben did a Google search for "disabled driving instructor Oxfordshire" and we struck it lucky. A lovely man called Nick, who had an encyclopaedic knowledge of all things disabled and driving, took me for lessons.

***

Wednesday 1st September 2010

I failed my driving test today! I guess I've never learnt to live through failure. The old Faiza was too damn perfect at everything. She passed her driving test first time and never failed at anything. Well, it's an important lesson for life, I guess. Well, my new life. I'm going to have to learn (or re-learn!) all the lessons that everyone learns as part of normal growing up.

But, maybe it's like puberty: the tallest kids are ones who have their growth spurts in late adolescence, because they're starting from bigger base height, and end up taller adults.

Or maybe that's just what I used to tell the short-arse 12 year-olds, to kid them into thinking that they won't be midgets for the rest of their lives.

Nick was keen to encourage me and to make sure that I get more lessons to prep me up for my next test. He told me he thinks I'll make it in the end.

Ben was quite nice, but it still wasn't what I wanted to hear. He said he thought that the DVLA were quite quick to book me an assessment. He was saying how he would have liked it if they'd given me a bit longer. I said, "Even longer!?"

Later, I was talking to Ami on the phone and she provided the yin to balance Ben's "take things slowly" yang. She was really surprised to hear that I'd failed. She certainly was not of the "I can't believe the DVLA assessed you so quickly" school of thought. I guess she only ever hears my version of how things are going. And maybe I only present quite a distorted view of how things are. Perhaps I'm a classic example of a "difficult head injury victim" and I can't see the reality outside of my own little, damaged brain.

***

I took weekly driving lessons for several months. A few weeks before the test, which I managed to pass, Nick took me for a driving lesson and left me with the words "If you drive like today on your assessment, they'll pass you, no problem."

I explained to him that this was not because 'something happened' over Christmas. I had simply reflected on my disability, learnt to accept it a bit more and stopped trying to drive the way the 'old Faiza' would have. Acceptance, I learnt, would ultimately play a crucial role not in overcoming my impairments, but in living a life in my new disabled body.

***

Wednesday 5th January 2011

I had a driving lesson today. Nick was saying that my driving has improved loads. I've got my test in a couple of weeks, so maybe he was just saying it to boost my confidence. I felt like I drove really badly today, but I think that's actually a good sign!?

Anyway, now Nick says that I'm like a new woman: accepting that I need to drive slower. My brain isn't this beast that I need to battle with and rein in any more. It's kind of like an NQT [Newly Qualified Teacher]. The secret is to stop wanting to "control the kids" and think of it more as "managing student behaviour".

I've stopped being so black-and-white about the whole thing. Old Faiza vs. Brain-damaged Siddiqui. I can see value in that little phrase that used to wind me up: they're just different. But I wouldn't want to get carried away with it: it's still my crap hand, not my "differently-abled hand".

Wednesday 23rd February 2011

I passed my driving test!! It's only an automatic, so not up to the "old Faiza" pass mark yet, but who gives a crap about that anyway? So that's one thing I can tick off my list now.

The thing is I don't know where I'm going with this newfound freedom. Maybe this is one of my "cognitive impairments". I never understood that not being able to drive wasn't really what made me 'housebound'. Really I was only housebound because I could never think of anywhere to go!

22 Reasonable Adjustments

Saturday 21st November 2009

Lad and Fran came over for dinner today. When Ben was in the kitchen cooking his masterpiece (he's quite good in that department now) they asked me about going back to work. I told them about how the insurance money means there aren't any big worries in that department. Fran joked about how it was kind of like winning the lottery.[126] It's really made me think, what's making it so hard for me when I'm being paid to sit at home and just be disabled?

I guess nothing. But there is the knowledge that I'm not as clever as I used to be. I didn't think I ever really thought I was THAT clever. Or at least I didn't think that I prided myself on being clever – that was part of who Faiza was. Everyone learns to accept who they are over time and I guess that I'd kind of accepted where I was in the big scheme of things: what I had and what I lacked. I'd already had quite a hard time becoming happy with my place in the world, I'm not looking forward to doing it again, and what if it doesn't work out?

But at the moment there's no reason to get up in the morning. Before, even though I used to get stressed out with the kids and all the pointless paperwork would get on top of me sometimes, I HAD to get out of bed, because I had to physically be in my classroom at 8:45 or we wouldn't be able to pay the mortgage.

But there was also the illusion that my existence was being used on something meaningful: something to use my brain on. I don't know what things were like at Summertown College, but I do remember lying awake at night sometimes, when I was at Heath Secondary. Sometimes this would be worrying about something stupid like Tina Palmer mouthing off at me in front of the other kids, but sometimes it would be because of some banal learning activity I got unnecessarily excited over.

I feel like that there must be something wrong with me. I'm in the minority of people who can't even be happy winning the lottery. But they do say that people who win loads of cash in the lottery end up depressed because the money doesn't bring them happiness and takes them away from their friends.

---

[126] We were aware how cruel that might sound amongst people who do not share our sense of humour, but all the people who were there understood the way in which it was meant and knew the extent to which Fran is kind, loving and understanding.

I want to have a meaningful job to show people that I do still have a brain. People like those crap OTs see how disabled one of the damaged bits is, and extrapolate this ineptitude across my whole psyche.

***

Tuesday 1ˢᵗ December 2009

… I had to do a million trial runs with Nicki, Ben and the OTs so I could go to the Headway day centre "independently", but I think I finally feel like a useful member of society again. I went to take this mosaic class there. I just helped the members there to make coasters, but they seemed to really enjoy it. I think I can learn a lot from them.

It was good to see other crips and see what they're going through. I went along quite arrogantly thinking "<u>I</u> am going to help <u>THEM</u>." But they've been crippled for a bit longer than I have, so their attitudes are quite different. I guess a bit more accepting. And they weren't arrogantly thinking things like "Why am I spending my time creating this pointlessly decorative coaster?" They just got down to it.

I sometimes feel like my life's a bit pointless, but what right do I have to feel like that? Is it alright for them to get satisfaction from things like this, but not for me? Why, because they're proper crips? Would I call their lives pointless? Well, no, so maybe I should take my head out of my own backside?

OK, I can't make it to the day centre without a million hours of labour from able-brained people and the old Faiza would have just driven there with the A to Z on her lap, but we have what we have. I think I will try to do lots of voluntary work. Maybe Ben's right about that.

Friday 27th August 2010

For the last few weeks I've been thinking about that Viktor Frankyl book. And since doing those mosaic classes with Headway, I've been kind of inspired to do more voluntary work. I emailed the Oxfordshire hospice about doing voluntary work there. I had my interview with them today. It was so good. It seems like a nice place with a really positive mentality, which is not something you'd expect from a hospice. But from what I saw on their website made them seem like a really kind and lovely place. Kind of like the OCE: has all these crips, but still believes that they can bring stuff to the world.

Anyway, they emailed back a few weeks ago, asked for my CV and wanted me to go in for an interview. I remember talking to David [Ben's dad] about telling people that I'm disabled, and he advised against it, especially in a work context, giving discrimination as his reason. So, I quoted the DDA[127] [Disability Discriminations Act] at him. And he said that that's just what the law says SHOULD happen, but in his experience, as a manager, it never actually does. He did that whole father thing of doling out advice, then acting like I'm being idealistic whenever I disregard his middle-aged "wisdom".

Anyway, I had an interview with the hospice today and it went really well. The fact that I'm a crip might have actually worked in my favour, because it means that I can relate to their crips better. (I was careful not to use the word "crip" in the interview though. It's kind of like someone who's mixed-race saying "us nigger bros" – might be a tad offensive.)

They did point out that I don't have THAT much in common with their crips, because they're heading towards the end, whereas I'm always getting better and better. Hmm. Good point.

They were so nice at the interview. FINALLY, somewhere where my talents are recognised. They even had printed out three more job descriptions that they wanted me to apply for, because they looked at my CV and thought that they could make good use of someone as skilled I am. It felt so good for someone to look at all the talents that I do have and what I could bring, but at the same time are fully aware of the crip side of me.

Anyway, they just need to do a CRB. [128] So, hopefully I'll be working there before the next century!

Tuesday 12 October 2010

I've been going to the Oxfordshire hospice training days. I really feel like I agree with their philosophy. I was talking to Najma on the phone and she'd heard of them before. She said how she likes them too and thinks they have a wonderful philosophy. I feel like when I start to work for them, my life could start to have a point.

And on the training days they addressed the fact that some people are put off because they think "Well, what's the point in putting so many resources into a life that is just going to end soon anyway?" And they kind of answered that by saying that you make a

---

127 The DDA is the disability discrimination act. It aims to protect disabled people and prevent disability discrimination, outling that any candidate for a job should have the right to employment and candidates can expect "reasonable and appropriate adjustments" to be made.

128 The Home Office website claims that CRBs should take 10 days, but in my experience it always took several months. They have got better: it only takes about a month and a half now.

difference to that individual, for that moment. Does it matter if their life is one that ends in sorrow? Isn't death part of life anyway? Do lives have less value because they aren't lived up to the full?

So, you might see a person reading Wordsworth and could think that the book in their hand isn't a waste of the rainforest because Wordsworth has been printed on it. But what if it was just the Argos catalogue? Surely everyone thinks that's a waste? But take this person reading Wordsworth — what if we THINK it's being appreciated in all its glory, when really there's just some brain-dead cripple gazing at it blankly? And would we say the same if this same person was reading the Argos catalogue? And what if this person reading Wordsworth was a philistine, who couldn't even tell the difference between Wordsworth and Argos?

Can we really claim that all life is equally meaningful? What does it mean to live in the moment, when the moment is just a brain-dead vegetable, staring blankly at a wall before hurtling towards death like a comet in cold space?

And what if that same someone needs massive sums of tax payers' money to be put on the fire, just to keep make sure they're warm even though they can't sense temperature? And then there's me using up loads of resources (inflicting myself on Ben, the NHS, friends and family). No one can really say that I live life in all its glory. I can't watch a good arty film or a witty comedy without Ben having to pause it and explain the jokes that go way over my head. Where do you draw the line?

I guess I can't kill myself because I'm (inshAllah) going to get better. But what if I don't? And what does this all mean about my life now? Do I just live for the glorious day when the old Faiza shall return?

Friday 29th October 2010

The Oxfordshire hospice invited me in for a meeting today. I was thinking on the bus how it'd be a good chance to talk about adaptations they could make for me. I don't know, but maybe they could keep more in-depth notes and have it centrally located at a place I could check before my meetings with one of their patients.

It did cross my mind that it's a bit strange how they chose to call me in for a meeting timed conveniently in the week after the training for all their general staff and before they start training for people who are actually going to work with their patients. And it turns out I wasn't just being paranoid — they sacked me in this meeting! And it was because I'm disabled! They were very careful not to say anything that could cause offence, but that in no way softened the blow. That's always the way with these things — people go all quiet, while I go crazy knowing there's something awful round the corner. Leaving me to figure out something incredibly head fucky with my mashed-up little brain. That's the kindest way: to endlessly beat about the bush.

This has not helped with my paranoia about white society trying to stop me getting ahead. Quite why I need to be kept out of a hospice, I don't know. Maybe I'd form a little crips union. Maybe THEIR patients are other people who white society has convinced not to take an active, and therefore dangerous, role in society. I don't know, but it all smells very fishy to me.

How convenient: their sacking me after selling themselves to me over four evenings so that I fall in love with them and their philosophy. Only THEN do they sack me, because "I'm too disabled" to work for them. With a bunch of crips! And they were using that to claim their patients are so impaired that they couldn't possibly risk inflicting someone like me on them. When I asked "so how would my impairments be problematic?" they couldn't give me an answer. I then foolishly added "I understand about my memory, but you could make "necessary and appropriate adaptations"". [129]

But, they'd obviously made up their minds: it's just too much hassle to accommodate a crip with a weird collection of incomprehensible impairments. They might actually have to stop and think when it's much easier to run on auto-pilot.

---

[129] "Reasonable and appropriate adaptations" is the phrase that I misquoted here. It is from the Disability Discrimination Act that I had become very familiar with while researching my return to employment.

23 The Haunting Mirror

Tuesday 6th October 2009

Val came round and asked me about what kind of voluntary work I wanted to do. And then she asked if I'd prefer to do it for other people with head injuries. I said I don't see why I should be interested in that especially. OK, I've had one, but does that mean I can't be interested in anything else?

I get annoyed with people like her always harping on about me "accepting my disability". That's just what they want, isn't it? I mean, why should I just accept it? And the way they all say it makes it sound like that's what's in my best interests. I admit the accident was a huge deal (not for me because I slept through it all and can't remember the worst bits, but for Ben). Can't we just say that it was just a single incident? Why should I let it dictate what happens to me forever more?

I hate that "accepting it" bollocks. Makes it sound like that's the healthy thing to do. I can't really deny that I was in that car crash. But isn't it more healthy to move on? You shouldn't let a single traumatic incident define who you are for the rest of your life.

I resent the idea that I'm in some sort of denial. What about those of us who don't have tissue paper for skin? And there's a sort of implication that if I was weaker and used a single incident as a crutch for my identity, then in some way I'd be more sorted.

***

Shortly before the accident I started the hobby of mosaicing. Back then, I had mosaiced a small table top, two plant pots and had procured a mirror that I was planning to frame with a handmade mosaic mirror frame. I had put aside sketches of my vision of the finished product in a storage cupboard by the mirror, and some wood that I had cut specifically for this purpose.

***

Saturday 28th November 2009

... That mirror sits there haunting me. It says "I've been here for nearly a year, why am I not finished? You're sooo slow!" I've tried to explain to it that I've been ill. But it just reminds me that I've been released from hospital for some time now, so there's no excuse. I should stop wallowing. OK, I'm off sick, but make the most of it now and use this time to do something productive.

I've been emailing round to try and start some voluntary work. I just feel like my life's such a waste. I do so little – I can't claim that I don't have enough time, can I?

Nicki [from Headway] said something about giving some of their members some mosaic classes. She said she'd go with me on the bus to their day centre, so I can learn the route.

***

The rest of 2009 and most of 2010 passed by slowly. I had been referred back to the OCE. I did some volunteer work. I watched TV and when I had the initiative I would clean the house.

***

Wednesday 21st July 2010

Hannah came round today to discuss voluntary work with me. I told her about all the problems there had been and she said that I might be able to do some at the OCE for them. Sounds quite good. But I do kind of want to move on with my life. I remember once in the upper limb group, this woman came in as an out-patient. The OT introduced her and said "This is so-and-so. She was a patient here 10 years ago." Then they both laughed, saying something like "You never get out of here." And I thought "Well, I'm getting out of here. Nothing's going to bring me back, no matter how functionally disabled my upper limb gets, I don't want to come back." But it looks like that's where I'm going to have to volunteer now.

Well, they said that I need to see the head of their volunteer team to talk about what's best for me. So, maybe they won't hire me either.

Tuesday 12th October 2010

I started voluntary work at the OCE today. I had to go in and meet the new patients and see what I could do. It was so weird. Everyone looked SO disabled. I don't remember it *being like that!* [130] *Maybe it's just this current batch of patients. But I asked the OTs what they thought of this batch and they seemed to be saying that there's nothing unusual about this lot, they're just like all the other ones.*

So, I've been left thinking "I must have been like that once." Maybe I was. And all the times that I can remember are just from when my brain was good enough to make memories, which I guess matches with when I was less crippled. I suppose that kind of explains why people were always so overjoyed with the progress I'd made whenever they saw me. They were just pleased to see me lift up a glass to my lips, because that was a big thing. Fucking hell: lifting up a glass was a big achievement.

It makes sense now when people say "you look so much better", I guess I must do. But it's weird that I don't know what's "wrong" with the patients there now: they just look odd. Like there was this one girl/woman in her 30s who acted like she was a big kid. When I told Ben about her, he said that it sounds like me when I first got there. Really?

---

[130] I wasn't able to recall that other patients were disabled. I have thought about this extensively, and after lots of reading have come to the conclusion that it was probably because of reduced insight caused by damage to my mirror neurones. The explanation is a bit involved, so let me start at the beginning...

Mirror neurones can be found in the brains of most animals. They are stimulated both when an animal acts and when the animal observes the same action being performed by another. The neurone "mirrors" the behaviour of the other, as though the observer were acting itself. These mirror neurones underlie animals' ability to empathise with what another is feeling or doing. This is not just a matter of emotional empathy, but suggests a basic mental mimicry of others – even down to their physical movements – that accompanies the passive reception of information at the basis of an animal's observation of the world. These neurones are especially developed in humans, and it has been suggested that this is what underlies our social natures.

Professors Giacomo Rizolatti and Vilayanur Ramachandran studied the interaction between anosognosia and these neurones.

Although many in the scientific community have doubts over their theory, they suggest that damage to them from a head injury can give us an explanation for some patients' reduced insight into the disabilities of others. Patients with damage to the mirror neurones do not mentally 'mirror' another person's movements – they do not empathise with them – and are not therefore in a position to form a judgement about whether or not the other person is moving normally, or is disabled. Whether others are having difficulties or not is just not on their radar. This must have been me. That's the best explanation that I have been able to find for why I don't remember my fellow patients at the OCE being especially ill.

Tuesday 7ᵗʰ December 2010

I'm quite enjoying it all at the OCE. I help out at "the social group". It's just a few patients with loads of different impairments. I'm finding it all quite interesting. For example, there was this guy there who would say "yeah" to everything. And he might say it angrily or with a laugh, but it would always be "yeah, yeah yeah."

You'd ask him a question like "do you want to put it in your bag or on you wheelchair?" And he'd say "yeah, yeah, yeah." He'd said that to everything. He obviously knew there was something wrong because his "yeah"s would get more and more frustrated with these thickos around him who'd refused to understand what "yeah" meant.

When it ended I talked to the speech and language therapist and she said how it's called expressive asphasia. [131] *I wrote the word down and I Googled it when I got home. That kind of explained it. Was it wrong that I found it interesting? What would Jesus do? Pity them? I guess he'd do a miracle and make them better. And I guess that's what the OCE's doing. It's just that neurological healing doesn't work as quickly as holy water.*

I do feel bad because I took a perverse pleasure in treating his disability as a form of entertainment. I guess it's better than the people who annoy me by turning a blind eye and pretending there's nothing wrong with me. Or that I just make up what's wrong with me. Can't concentrate? Well, focus harder! Not that anyone ever says that. No, it's better just to act like it. Or pretend that there's nothing really the matter.

I guess that's what pity is: people compensating for a lack of holy water. And we couldn't possibly change ourselves to address the problem they remind us of. No, that would be a step too far. But I guess that's what the OCE's doing. 'Enabling': teaching the cripple to live in an able-bodied world. I guess they're saying that the world should make 'reasonable adjustments' too.

But what is reasonable? Surely you're not suggesting that I'm asking people to engage their brains? No. That's not reasonable: expecting thought from an able brained person. Why should THEY think? They are the lucky ones. No, it's much better to pity.

---

[131] Aphasia is an umbrella term for acquired language disorders, where the pathways for language comprehension or production are disrupted from an injury to the left hemisphere of the brain. To briefly summarise, this patient's speech was perfectly articulated, but his difficulty with language was rooted in an impaired ability to locate the correct words to express an idea. (He did not have an impaired ability to reason, simply to express himself.) *The Man Who Lost His Language* explores a similar case in much more detail than I have the space or expertise for.

Tuesday 14th December 2010

I went to social group. We all made some Christmas cards. I'm finding it all quite difficult. I think I've been a bit cocky thinking "I've had a brain injury. So, I know EVERYTHING about them. Certainly more than all you know-it-all OTs."

There was this patient there called Clare. Clare had a stroke, which left her left-hand crapified but she was left handed. She's not at all cognitively impaired, which means she's 100% aware what's wrong with her and uses the sessions to get better.

I think I've always been quite cocky about this incredible recovery that I've apparently made. And I've put it all down to how I was always so upbeat and determined. But seeing Clare, it's dawned on me that I was not someone to be admired: I was just so positive because I was oblivious to the fact that I wouldn't be back to 100%. I never realised that I'd have to live for years, decades, being 60%, 80%, 95%. Whenever I've realised just how crippled I am, I've been anything but upbeat.

Here's Clare totally aware of what's wrong with her and determined to do the work to get better. When she wrote out her Christmas card to her son with her right hand I said, "You're lying, you were right-handed all along" as a joke – I think I was determined not to give her a patronising "Well done, you've written that out so neatly." She got all angry and said that she's been working on her right hand really hard for months and that's why it looked so neat. I had to quickly back track and say "Of course you have been, it's just that it looks so amazing you can barely tell." Except, that you could tell - it looked like a crip had written it. I can't believe I was so patronising!

But she's totally aware of what her impairments are, and worked through them systematically to be more "normal".

Tuesday 11th January 2011

Went to social group the other day and I find it quite good to see how different people react to their disabilities. I was all inspired before to see people who worked hard to make themselves more normal, but I think I've taken that too far, thinking "if you want to get better then it's got to be hard work, which is unpleasant."

But not everyone chooses the hard slog to be more normal. There was a much older lady who had had a stroke and there were no massive cognitive problems. She just seemed to be a bit more resigned to being an old lady and all the bodily problems that go with that. She just seemed to accept the cards that Allah had dealt her.

Maybe it's got something to do with being older and wiser? Or maybe it's just more pragmatic because people who are older tend to not recover as well as someone in their 20s or 30s. Maybe the older you are the more you accept your mortality, compared with someone who's got their whole life ahead of them? Maybe they're just two sides of the same coin.

I guess people just cope however they do. There's no right or wrong.

24 Career

I went to Summertown's Christmas concert thing today. It got me thinking about going back to work. I don't see why I can't. People always ask me if I remember my physics. They just don't seem to get that even though I can remember the lifecycle of a star, I still have a shit memory. Frank [a teacher I used to work with] used to have an awful memory, but no one ever asked him if he remembers his physics. The only difference is that he was born with a crap memory, whereas mine is an 'acquired impairment'.

Ben's convinced me that it's in 'my best interests' to wait a bit longer before I go back to work there. I guess I should at least pass my driving test before I go back. But I can get the 25 [bus] and then take driving lessons on weekends. So, he's agreed that maybe I should try going back not next September but the September after that. That'll be September 2011!! And that's only on a part time basis because of 'my fatigue'! Well, I guess when I'm not at school I can do lots of stuff to put on my CV. Like voluntary work and general academic stuff in science education.

***

The scene is a living area off the side of a very tidy kitchen tiled in grey with a black settee at which Carol and Faiza are sitting with a TV on quietly in the background.

CAROL: We went by Nanny and Grandad's last night to watch that football match...

FAIZA: Oh, yeah? Was it a big match?

CAROL: [thinking]. Man U versus Real Madrid.

FAIZA: How are they?

CAROL: Oh, yeah they're well. That flu really took it out of Nanny, though.

FAIZA: Did Steve come by too?

CAROL: [quizzical look]

FAIZA: Just 'cause he normally comes by if the football's on.

CAROL: Oh, no. He didn't come for this one. But we did see him last week.

FAIZA: Oh yeah?

CAROL: He was telling me about his friend.

FAIZA: Oh, yeah, the one who had a diffuse axonal injury?

CAROL: [with curiosity] Yeah. He's much better now. But it took him a good ten
         years to get back to work.

FAIZA: Yeah, it CAN take a really long time.

CAROL: But now he said you wouldn't even know. He said even if you had to
         look out for it you wouldn't be able to tell.

FAIZA: No?

CAROL: Steve said he's totally normal now.

FAIZA: [cautiously] Hmm. That's good.

CAROL: It'll take time, but there is hope that you should make it.

FAIZA: Yeah, I do kind of know that I should be able to go back into something,
         it's just what and when.

**

Various people often reassured me that I am not 'properly disabled'. Looking back, they were almost certainly well-intentioned, preferring not to dwell on the negative, focusing more on what I *could* do. In my more unforgiving moments, I thought of it as people preferring not to be reminded of the pain in their own lives. They probably just found it easier to ignore the elephant in the room that was my disability.

But then people at the other extreme would also annoy me: the therapists could not see beyond this elephant. They seemed to exclusively focus on how best to manage my disability. That was, after all, what they were paid for. But I was left feeling that living my life somehow took second place to behaving in a manner appropriate to my condition.

All the time, I felt as though I was being constantly compared to a textbook example of the ideal disabled woman. She had also suffered a diffuse axonal injury but chose to deal with it in the right way. She was willing to accept her disability, without entertaining any arrogant, paranoid delusions about how she was ready to go back to work. She successfully managed her impairments using all the suggested adaptations.

On the one hand I was often being told (sorry... reassured) that I am not properly disabled, and on the other that I should just accept my disability. Often I would congratulate myself on how strong I was, when everyone seemed to act as though accepting "the disability" was a major task. After all, there wasn't really anything to accept. But I could never really trust what they were saying, because there did seem to be something up. And it seemed that the closer I was to someone the more they seemed to behave as though there was something wrong.

While I wrestled with these contradicting attitudes, my cognitive abilities had developed so that I had become increasingly adept at using the internet. The 'net was its own bottomless pit of advice. 'Accepting the disability' was something that people like me were heavily encouraged to do. Unsurprisingly, this fed the growing beast of my paranoia. It seemed only logical to me that it would be in the interests of white society to persuade me to accept my "disability". According to them, I should stop dreaming of a life that has some kind of higher purpose. So I always took their advice with a kilo of salt, while submitting quietly to their claims that I would not be able to "function" independently.

Unsurprisingly, this theoretical, textbook ideal of how to deal with disability appeared to me as someone white. I have had numerous conversations/arguments with Ben, where he has tried to convince me that my feelings of alienation are not explicitly rooted in race. He tells me that Marx[132] would see them as a manifestation of the alienation that I experience from a capitalist society. At best, I can be persuaded that it is a coalescence of the various forms of disenfranchisement that I feel: this ideal woman was everything I could not be.

Of course I hated the idea of accepting my "disability", but as the months passed by I realised that despite my best efforts to not make adaptations, I had already started modelling my life on this ideal woman. My day would run much better if I carried water and some aspirin with me. I hated to say it, but my functioning was better if I paced myself and did not attack tasks in the same way that I thought that old Faiza would have.

---

[132] I should remind the reader that Ben is something of a Marxist.

As I began living my new and adapted life, I recalled a conversation that I had with Naveed a little while ago. While we were chatting about something or other, his phone interrupted us with a text message beep. Once he had checked what the message was, we restarted the conversation from where we had left off. He commented on how much better I had got.

Now, to the outsider this might not seem like anything to write home about, but what Naveed pointed out was that this ability to take up the thread of a conversation again without being distracted, was not something I would have been capable of even a few months earlier. For me, this rang true. I started to see exactly why it was called the 'invisible disability': here was something so tiny, but with potentially massive consequences for your life if you can't do it. Not just restarting a conversation from where you left off, but losing your train of thought when the wind blows or the phone rings, and the world falling away from your feet as you fight to remember what you were doing.

Naveed's comments helped me to finally see this 'invisible disability', which the establishment (the object of my paranoia) claimed prevented me from returning to work. It was no longer quite as unknown as it had been. Naveed concluded, "I don't know if you'll go back to teaching specifically, but what I can say is that you won't be dependent on this insurance money in the long run," adding, "You are getting better all the time."

Around this time people would often compliment me, saying things like "You've got so much better since I last saw you", or "It's lovely to see you looking so well." I was left utterly disoriented. I would think, "I didn't think anything was wrong with me before." This became such a frequent occurrence, that this thought was always followed by another: "They'll probably say the same thing when I see them in a few months' time. So what does that say about what's wrong with me now?" I experienced this kindness as not much more than a secret insult. After Naveed's intervention, I started to see what they might mean.

Having understood that I did have impairments, and why they might be invisible, I started to understand what people meant when they advised me to 'accept my disability'. It stopped being something I hated, just rolling over and accepting that I was a worthless sponge on the able-bodied. Instead, it meant living each moment that Allah gave me, and finding hope within it. Not making the most of the abundant talents that the old Faiza had, but achieving new things with my crippled self. Just living: flowing between submission and hope.

I had already accepted that I believed in an all powerful creator. Now, I had to acknowledge that He had chosen this for me. Submit to the reality of my disability. Accept it: whatever its course. Engaging with what was wrong with me was at the heart of 'getting better', or getting the most out this new body that Allah had given me.

At the end of this cascade of thoughts that Naveed had prompted, I began to concentrate more on my career and my eventual return to work. I became less fixated on the narrow goal of getting 'well' again, and began to think about living a life which, even if I did not consider it to be normal, was happy living. A life which, until then, had been the property of the "old Faiza". I began to appreciate just what neurological healing was, and the excruciatingly slow rate at which it would have to take place. I decided that while I was waiting for the old Faiza to return, I had better start making 'adaptations', to make living a pleasant experience.

I began to think about my career, and about what might suit me best. But exactly what that might be began to bother me less. I had already discarded a lot of career choices because I was living in the shadow of the old Faiza. A Cambridge graduate, I had told myself, should do a lot better. Now, I was happy just to live my life.

A few weeks later I received an email from one of my MA lecturers from King's College. (How Convenient pointed out to me just how lucky it was that I had done an MA in education.) It invited me to 'cafe ASE': a talk given by different prominent academic figures within the field of science education. It is attended mainly by secondary science teachers and is linked with the Association of Science Educators. It meets every month in a Waterstone's bookshop just a few minutes' walk from Euston Square tube station, by King's College.

After I had become excited at the idea of attending this talk, I realised that, even though I passed this Waterstone's almost every day for a year on my way to the library or to lectures, I had forgotten where it was because of my retrograde amnesia. So the day before the talk, I printed off a map of the route from the tube station to Waterstone's, and annotated it with directions and put it ready in my stripey 'leaving the house bag'.

This is a bag that I bought from a street trader in Delhi when on holiday with Ben. In order to help me cope with my memory problems, I would keep it packed with everything I would need whenever I left the comfort zone of my house. That way I would only ever have to remember one item: my bag.

It is a tough yellow and red striped bag adorned with a variety of handy pockets, each with that classic feature of Indian street traders' designs: a cheap zip that broke within days of its purchase. It always sits in the hallway and is packed with my various 'essentials': my keys, mobile, wallet, my "pensioner's bus pass", a paperback and my iPod.

I would 'lose' my mobile at least a dozen times a month on my twice weekly exercise on prescription trips to the leisure centre. On each trip there would be periodic moments of panic. In order to help me to cope with this, I gave each of the various "zipped" pockets a name and allocated a specific item to it. The small pocket inside the main, large one is called 'the secret pocket'. It is secret, because it was hard for opportunist pickpocketers to access without my knowledge. As a result it has been instated as home to my wallet.

Another one of the pockets with an assigned name and function is a zip-less pocket on the outside of the bag. Its presence is more visible and easily accessible to pick pocketers. As a result, it never merited the title 'secret'; it was merely 'quiet'. And because it did not possess even a broken zip, I saw it not as a pocket, merely a 'flap'. This region of the bag was thus christened the 'quiet flap'. It contains an eye patch, so that I could pull it out whenever I had to read something quickly. And then there is my Oyster card, so that I could access it quickly, without incurring the wrath of busy commuters. They would not take too kindly to being held up by a crip who was cack-handedly rooting around for her Oyster card in an inappropriately overfilled bag.

I also put in a pen and some paper for any notes that I wanted to make. I could use it to jot down questions if they sprang into my injured head during the talk. This is a strategy that I had developed to let me concentrate without forgetting a valuable thought. Also, because I can suffer from headaches when dehydrated, I keep an old Coke bottle in this bag which I filled up with water. And because I can go a little 'peculiar' if my blood-sugar level drops, my bag also harbours what I call an 'emergency banana'.

With both classic head injury affectation and typical Faiza style, I began getting myself ready for leaving the house 5 minutes after an organised person would have left. It was only when Ben asked me "what sort of people will be at this thing?", that it occurred to me that a pair of combats and the indie-style retro T-shirt that I was wearing, might not be the most appropriate clothes to wear to an academic talk. So I hastily wrapped around myself a full length black coat, which was bought for me last Christmas. I also grabbed my Selwyn College scarf, which effectively said to anyone I might need to schmooze with and impress: "This brain damaged cripple might not know how to dress herself, but she went to one of the top universities in the country, you know."

I caught a coach from Oxford to London, which is a route that I have taught my 'new brain'. It is an incredibly simple route straight along the M40/A40 that I feel comfortable on, always able to confront panic by just looking out of the window for a few minutes until we pass a road sign that tells us how far along the straight route we are. Once I make it to a London underground station, I can successfully navigate my way to anywhere in Zone 1 because the tube map had been hardwired into my brain a long time ago. (The old Faiza had lived in London since she was born and, like all Londoners, had an embarrassing degree of familiarity with the underground map.)

It was the first time in a long while that I had been out by myself walking through London. I walked from Euston Square tube station, with the stripey leaving-the-house bag slung over my shoulder. Like most middle-agers, my taste in music was stuck to what all the rage was when I was a teenager, and I relived my youth by listening to Blur's *Parklife* on my iPod.

The 'crap OTs' still managed to force their way into my thoughts. I smugly thought about how I would tick one of their boxes by demonstrating independence, even though I knew they would tell me off for having headphones on whilst walking down a busy London Road, when I am as disabled as they think I am.

Full of intellectual excitement, I felt rejuvenated, re-entering the world of education. I felt so glad that I had decided to go to cafe ASE. It had made me feel alive, just by being around people who I share an interest with. (For them, it was an interest about the way that children learn science; for me it was an interest in how damaged brains work.)

Because of my schooling and general upbringing, I could not help but consider this from the perspective of my CV. I felt that something within science education would be the right choice to make. If nothing else, I should be able to convince any potential employers that my years of working as a secondary school teacher were not a waste, but had given me a massive wealth of relevant experience observing first-hand how children make sense of physics.

So, I walked down the road, away from cafe ASE, feeling a bit smug about myself. If I hadn't "successfully managed" all of my impairments, I had definitely learned to adapt myself to the live a life that a head case, like myself, should be grateful for. I could see the sun setting, as I walked down the ordered chaos that is Euston Road, inhaling the exhaust fumes.

25 Moon Beauty Appreciation

I could no longer rely on my own memories: they all seemed so vague, and were disturbingly different from other people's recollections. But I could not plan for tomorrow either: I had no idea what the future would look like. I knew that I should get better, but there was nothing wrong with me now, so what did that even mean?

I had heard about the Buddhist idea of living in the present moment. This seemed appropriate for someone with no memories, but I could not even do that: I was unable to read or even watch a film. So, what could I do? I knew that I SHOULD be grateful to Allah for giving me this life that they refer to as a gift. This motivated me into doing *salaat* [prayer[133]]. I did not want to stop worship, because that would somehow be ungrateful of me. I certainly did not want to appear thankless.

So I started to think more deeply about what it meant to be 'grateful to Allah'. How could I claim to be thankful for this life, when I had been making plans to bring an end to it? And why did Allah save me anyway? Surely not so that I could throw this life that he had 'blessed' me with right back in his face.

I felt that it would be just too clichéd to simply think of the car crash as some kind of punishment. And anyway, how would suicide square with my joke that "This bang on the head was just like pressing Ctrl, Alt, Delete on my brain"? I could not feel the despair that was all around me.

Back in August 2010 I wrote an email to Najma, berating this clichéd reaction to life-changing events as some sort of punishment from above. In this rant I included a link to a poem, written by Rumi. Rumi was a Sufi-Muslim mystic who lived in thirteenth century Persia. He is now best known for the beautiful poetry he wrote. I can't really remember what I understood of it, but it seems that it must have articulated something to me about this car crash. I had heard people refer to hardships as things that can be seen as blessings, and I think that for all my efforts at keeping my pain away from Allah, this shows that something similar was happening in me.

---

133 *Salaat* translates as 'worship'. It normally refers to the recitation of Arabic verses from the Qur'an which, in my case, I had already memorised as a child.

THE HOTEL

My life is just like a hotel;
Every morning a new arrival.

Joy; despair; some anger;
each fleeting mood arrives
like an unexpected guest.

Welcome and make friends them all!
Even crowding anguish
emptying your home of all possessions;
treat each with good grace.
They may be carving you out
for some new delight.

The evil thought, the guilt, the hatred;
meet them with kindness and ask them in.

Be grateful for every one of them.
Because each was sent
as a guide from heaven.

> *Jelaluddin Rumi,*
> *(my translation)*

This head injury gave me a chance to start again, and I started using my time off sick to have a good clear out.

***

The first thing I had to clear out was feelings about how inadequate my body was compared to "old Faiza's" perfect physique.

Monday 4th October 2010

I was talking to Carol and David about how technically I haven't got any disfiguring scars, but I still feel like my body's been mutilated. They just said that I look the same as I've always done.

So, what they're basically saying is that I'm as ugly as I've always looked! But that's the thing, my body's untouched. All the damage is quite literally in my head.

I know that there isn't actually anything particularly different about me. Now I realise the reason I look this disfigured in my mind's eye is because I FEEL like a cripple. But I don't think that I'm making it up – it all comes from the messages my brain's getting from my body. It just doesn't behave as it should: my balance is fucked. And my body's so unresponsive: it just doesn't sit right.

It's left me wondering: why do I feel like this? I'm not in THAT much pain. Do I have low self-esteem? Is it because I don't work? Or is it because I know that I'm a burden?

***

Ben pointed out to me later that his parents couldn't have said much else: if they had said that I don't look that bad, I would have felt that my thoughts were immediately discounted because they were brain damaged. I wouldn't be happy if someone had agreed with me and said that I was uglier than before.

True, there were no particular flaws in my appearance, but I did look different. Living under the rules of social interaction that I'm learning to live under, all they could say was "You do look just the same." No, I look brain damaged and more vacant.

So, talking to me about this is a bit of a lose-lose situation.

***

Friday 15th October 2010

I'm round at Ami's. Successfully killed time by watching How To Look Good Naked. It's made me think about how I would be the ideal person for them with my cripple story. They could start off about the "miraculous recovery" that everyone says I've made. Then I could say a bit about how I think of myself as having been hideously disfigured in the car crash, even though no one else says they see it.

Also, How To Look Good Naked buys you a whole new wardrobe for free! The price I'd have to pay would be being the object of other people's pity for 25 minutes with an advert break in the middle. People would be able to watch it and congratulate themselves on how confident they feel about themselves. Then they could pity the poor cripple, who has to have Gok Wan force her to believe in herself even though she looks shit.

I do think there is something wrong with me, though. Just the word "disabled" captures it: un-right.

It's true that everyone loves to feel sorry for this immense "tragedy" that happened to someone else. Then they can all pause their shiny, happy, functioning lives and think about:
a) how lucky they are (and therefore how unlucky this poor cripple is)
b) the fact that "it just goes to show that it COULD happen to any one of us." Except that it hasn't!

***

Wednesday 2oth October 2010

Had an appointment with Dr. H-S today. I talked to him about the fact that I don't orgasm anymore and then he asked me "Did you use to before?" I took the opportunity to crack a joke: "If I can get treatment for lack of orgasm on the NHS, then all women everywhere will expect the same and our health budget will go through the roof." He gave a nice, polite "ha."

Anyway, he's referred me to a psycho-sexual therapist. I didn't know that such people existed! I told him my little theory about how I thought that the bit of my brain that does orgasm had gone kaput and he said it's a bit more complicated than that. I think I sold my theory short by using such non-technical lingo...

***

A common difficulty faced by patients with neurological conditions is with relationships. Sexual problems are common to people who have survived a head injury, which is why the OCE has a relationship counsellor. Although damage to the hypothalamus is specifically associated with affected sexuality, it is important to remember that changes to a person's sexuality can rarely be fully explained by a single cause. As well as the sensitivity of the brain itself, the entire limbic system is crucial for experiencing orgasms. So, late in 2010 I was referred to Liz Ryan, the

OCE's psychosexual therapist. For me, she recommended a book with the title *Becoming Orgasmic.* [134]

In addition to discussions about how a woman's relationship with her body is central to her sexuality, the book outlines some exercises the reader can do for her own sexual growth. These ranged from answering questions that helped explore her formative ideas about sexuality, to actually physically exploring the body, and masturbating. Through this book I learnt about how the attitudes that I developed as a child sculpted my sexuality, and the ways that they had interacted with the 'anorgasmia' that I had experienced since the car crash.

The book asks the reader to focus on the actual sensations that her body experiences, rather than fixating on "how far away the orgasm is". (No woman has ever achieved orgasm by fixating on her distance from its arrival.)

***

Tuesday 8 February 2011

... I've been reading/doing Becoming Orgasmic *and it's getting really good. I've just done the first few chapters and it gets you to look at where your ideas about sex come from. It's pretty obvious when you think about it, but there is no such thing as an orgasm gland. It's all about how you feel about yourself. It turns out that my "anorgasmia" is because of problems I have with my self-image. I never realised that I had such low self-esteem...*

Tuesday 1ˢᵗ March 2011

... I also did an exercise in Becoming Orgasmic. *It told me to take a bath, then spend some time looking at my naked body. I needed to think about how I feel about the way I look. The exercise told me to shut my eyes while I was still in the bath and look at myself in my mind's eye. Then once out, I was supposed to look at myself in the full length mirror and compare it with the images I had of myself in my mind's eye. It's quite interesting comparing the two images: they're quite different. Does that automatically mean that I've got "low self-esteem"?*

In my mind's eye, I still picture myself like I was before I started my MA: I'm a young funky woman who's confident and quite attractive. Or at least that's how I think the "old Faiza" was. But at the same time I know that I can't be too confident with that image of

---

[134] *Becoming Orgasmic: A Sexual and Personal Growth Programme for Women* by Julia R. Heiman, Leslie Lo Piccolo and Joseph Lopiccolo.

myself, because I'm three years older and it feels like I have cobwebs over my whole body. (Or just the left side!)

With my actual eye, when I looked at myself in the mirror, I was not nearly as bad as I thought I looked. I looked at my tracheostomy and peg tube scars and they weren't as hideous as I thought they'd be. And although there were quite a few random scars all over my body, I was able to dismiss them knowing they're just shrapnel from the car or from random medical tubes the hospital put in.

I can look past all these scars, but the fact is that my body still just doesn't feel like it belongs to me. I have all these vague memories of physio sessions at the OCE, when they'd try to re-teach my brain how to control this body. Even though I have since graduated to the next level, it still feels a bit like it doesn't belong to me.

I guess it all feels like I'm a pathetic teacher whose kids just run around, trashing the classroom. This picture of my body is just based on the physical information it gives my brain. No wonder it thinks it's wrong. I feel like the "hazard elderly people crossing sign": all hunched over and the opposite of athletic.

Sunday 18th March 2011

It feels like everything that I'd thought before has been turned upside-down. Wanking is now a legitimate activity!

To put it in a way that is more socially acceptable, I've been working really hard on re-building our marriage: doing more of that Becoming Orgasmic book. It gets you to focus on your body and its sensations. It doesn't really matter that it's crippled, you can still feel the textures on your skin, whether it's spotty, silky-smooth or hairy. It kind of says it's all you and it's all allowed.

I know it sounds really obvious, but I think it needed saying.

It has a really good bit on one of my pet topics: how disability can be a gift. Someone who's had a mastectomy can actually be more sexy than Pamela Anderson. The boobless woman has had to learn that there's more to being a sexy woman than ample bosomage.

Then when I was on the phone to Najma and she politely asked "What have you been doing?" I had to omit all the gory details. People often politely ask me whether I have exercises to do (meaning physio or cognitive exercises). I don't think they mean wanking. But, it is part of my recovery. If my ultimate goal is to be like the old Faiza, then I have to "Become Orgasmic"...

***

Even though I was regaining ownership of my body, I still had to live in the real world and pass my driving test. Surely there was something wrong, as I had always been someone who achieved a lot in life without much effort. And yet now, at the age of 28, I was struggling to pass my driving test. What was wrong with me? If I wanted to live a happy life, I understood that I would have to just accept this. But I didn't want to. If I accepted this, what would be left of my life? Would it even be worth living?

When I was a teenager I used to feel as though I was a failure. I did not fit in at school and was always a disappointment to my family. They never said it explicitly, but like many overachieving teenagers I did not have to hear it to think that I fell short of the mark.

Then I 'got better' by throwing myself into my work and achieving yet more because CBT taught me that my way of coping with things was to achieve. I never had to accept myself for me, because I always forced myself to do better and conform more. I never had to confront these feelings until now. When achievement itself was the problem, I had no other way of coping. It felt like the rug had been pulled from under me.

Now that I could not achieve anything, was there any point to my life? No. But I could still 'achieve' *something*. I would have a big bowl of ice-cream and enjoy it. True, the old Faiza would have picked out some subtle flavours that I couldn't now, but it still tasted good. When having sex I could feel the texture of Ben's hand on the nape of my neck, even if I never "achieved" orgasm. I could still tell the old Faiza that I was achieving. I could still do something with my life, even if a Cambridge graduate should do better.

I have to learn to accept one of the remaining effects of my head injury at the more subtle end of the spectrum. I feel as though I am not as talkative and struggle to process conversation on the spot. Everyone reassures me that I am "no different". So, maybe I was always this slow witted?

When my head feels overloaded with sensory input, I want to shut my eyes and block it all out. But I have learned that if I do this people feel the need to express their concern. I do not take this well. So, I've learned to defocus my eyes or observe the angles that the vertices of a room make with the furniture. After a few minutes I am ready to play at being the 'old Faiza' again. This way, no one is alerted to the distressing presence of my damaged brain.

***

Monday 11th April 2011

Had a gorgeous couple of days. I went to stay at Wendy's. On my way from the station, I saw a beautiful full moon in the night sky as I was walking down some grotty east London high street. It was kind of like I was seeing a full moon for the first time ever. I had to walk from Bow Road station down "Addington Road" on the way to the flat. Normally I would have been saying "Addington Road, Addington Road, Addington Road" all the way there. But I didn't have to do that because my memory's got better. I could let my mind wander and look at the sky. The Moon leapt out at me. (It's been the first time the new Faiza's seen such a beautiful moon.)

In the eyes of an OT, it doesn't sound like I've made that much progress – but to me it all shows that I've got SO much got better. It's a HUGE thing for me, but because there's no box that they can tick for "Moon beauty appreciation", it's not on their radar, and is not seen as getting better.

It always used to freak me out when people said, "You seem so much better from when we last saw you." Really? I guess they must be picking up on stuff like "Moon beauty appreciation". And I wouldn't say there was something wrong with me because my Moon appreciation was below average, but that's kind of what was wrong with me.

What I want to know is: how did they know I had impaired Moon beauty appreciation? They're not in my head, are they? But, maybe that's why I wanted to kill myself?

They could never put that in a coroner's report, though. "Cause of death: impaired Moon beauty appreciation."

***

Then as the months, or years, passed by, my feelings about the head injury became mixed:

16 January 2012

I'm back from Manchester now. We went up for a Quran khani [religious gathering]. It was kind of nice seeing everyone. Aisha was there. She'd obviously heard about my accident and asked me how I am now and kept asking if I'm back at work yet. I didn't know what to say. Don't they know how that sounds? ("You look fine to me: why are you not working yet, you benefit cheat?")

But, I have to 'decentre' and consider it from their point of view. They're just saying it either out of curiosity or because they're trying to be nice. But what am I supposed to say? And to what extent should I lie about how I'm all fixed now?

Generally, I feel quite mixed, but one thing that I'm sure of is that people's reactions do still annoy me. Everyone feels the need to acknowledge that "it must have been hard for you". Yeah, a discrete unpleasant event that we can't talk about now because it's in the past. Actually it's been quite a nice thing. But I can't say that because "it's so hard". I probably wouldn't have chosen to crash the car, but it's not actually THAT bad. Yet I can't say that because everyone feels so sorry for me.

Would I have chosen it 3 years ago? No: I probably wouldn't have chosen to spend the rest of my life in this weird limbo, and I definitely liked being a teacher. (Well, more than a useless leech.) But do I love my crap brain now? Yes. It's liberated me from my old head: it used to be locked-in by the shackles of logic and executive functioning. It's a totally different way of seeing the world. Now Allah's given me new eyes. Or rather, he's given me a new occipital lobe! [135]

---

[135] The occipital lobe is the visual processing centre of the mammalian brain containing most of the anatomical region of the visual cortex.

Epilogue

I knew that I wanted to write something about the head injury around four years ago, when I was seeing the "crap OTs". I found it really hard to type, and even harder to stick with a thought for more than a few minutes. But at the same time, everyone was always telling me what a huge experience this was going to be. So I really wanted to spend some time writing about this.

I knew that there were other people out there like me: I had met them when I was in rehab, at the Headway day centre or, more recently, when I've been going to The Silverlining charity. My story, it would seem, was not so unique. (In fact, there are half a million people in the UK living with long term disabilities because of brain injuries.)

And if I was serious about this book then I knew that I had better get started, because I was always forgetting stuff. So whenever I sent emails, I made a special effort to talk about what I really felt. (Essentially, I ranted to whoever I could.) Sometimes I sent these emails to myself, so that I would have a genuine record of these "traumatic" events. I guess that was my diary.

I wanted to make sure that this book was going to be straight from the cripple's mouth and this is my attempt to capture what I thought and what I felt. My thoughts weren't less profound, though for being a cripple's. The accident hadn't made me stupid.

What's more, everyone was always telling me how much I was improving. Soon if everything went well I would cross over the fence and join them in the paradise of white society. All going well, this voice would be lost forever.

Now, it's been over five years since the car crash (and two since I finished this memoir). I found that time frustrating because my world was filled with superiors, so my voice was never heard. They always knew what was best for me. Over time I have had to swallow the bitter pill that in lots of ways they really did know better.

When I started out, this book was going to be a memoir of the "amazing recovery" that everyone said I was making. Then, gradually I started to mature. It slowly dawned upon me that this is not just my recovery – it belongs to all the people around me. Being surrounded by loving people and having specialist care helped things I could never have done on my own. We all had to learn, or are having to learn, that rehabilitation is not up to an individual: we all need to take ownership of whatever happens.

This book is also a celebration of the brain: it's amazing. True, it can never really fix itself completely. But it does have a tremendous ability to keep learning, which is why this book is one of hope. To me, hope used to be a barbed concept: one day, Insha'Allah, there will be a scientific breakthrough to fix my head. What I think was meant that the moment always has value, no matter how painful or undignified.

So, this book is a memoir of that time, and my process of learning to adapt to whatever this head throws my way. It was only through exploring these issues, properly, that I learned to have more grown up attitudes towards illness and recovery. It is only by engaging with this brain injury that I can lead the most fulfilling life that can be lead by someone like me.

This memoir looked at that head. She is going and this is all we'll have left of her.

Thank yous

There are lots of people I want to say thank you to.

I hope they all know who they are and that all their hard work and patience was gratefully received with a lot of love. So, thank you to everyone who took care of me after the accident: all the people who worked on the neurosciences ward in the JR and all the staff at the OCE (there are too many to mention individually); Nicki & Clair at Headway and Nicola & Maggie at The Silverlining, Oxford.

Thank you to all my friends, in particular everyone who read drafts of this book (especially Ben B., Chloe, Chris, Lara and Noreen). I really want to send a big thank you to Alex: your kindness and literary genius coalesced to make this whole thing work. I also want to say a special thank you to Kitty Wheater, whose incredibly thorough comments on my book went so far beyond the repayment of the favour that I cheekily asked it in exchange for!

And then there are the hundreds of people who listened to me pour my heart out and who still stick by me when I'm not really at my most fun. I also want to say thank you to my family for loving me no matter what I was or wasn't able to do. And for trekking out to Oxford to visit me. And to Ben's family for taking such good care of him, so he could be strong for me. And be here for me now.

And then to Ben.

Reading

Here are the full references of reading that I've mentioned as well as other books and factsheets that I (& people around me) have found interesting and useful.

Richard Bentall, *Madness Explained: Psychosis and Human Nature*. London: Penguin, 2004.

Molly Birnbaum, *Season to Taste: How I Lost My Sense of Smell and Found My Way*. London: HarperCollins, 2011.

Tony Buzan, *The Buzan Study Skills Handbook: The Shortcut to Success in Your Studies with Mind Mapping, Speed Reading and Winning Memory Techniques (Mind Set)*. London: BBC Active, 2006.

Care Quality Commission, *Count me in: Results of the 2009 national census of inpatients on supervised community treatment in mental health and learning disability services in England and Wales*. Retrieved 8th August 2012, from http://archive.cqc.org.uk/_db/_documents/Count_me_in_2009_(FINAL_tagged).pdf.

Havi Carel, *Illness*. Durham: Acumen Publishing, 2008.

Audrey Daisley, Rachel Tams & Udo Kischka, *Head Injury (The Facts)*. Oxford: University Press, 2009.

Antonio Damasio, *Descartes' Error: Emotion, Reason and The Human Brain*. London: Vintage, 1994

Marion Diamond, Arnold Scheibel & Lawrence Elson, *The Human Brain Colouring Book (Coloring Concepts Series)*. London: HarperCollins, 1985.

Dieter Ebert & Teri E. Klein, "Hallucinations as a side effect of venlafaxine treatment - a case report", in *Psychiatry On-line*. Retrieved 30/09/2013.

John Fleischman, *Phineas Gage*. New York: Houghton Mifflin Company, 2002.

Joshua Foer & Michel Siffre, "Caveman: An Interview with Michel Siffre," in *Cabinet Magazine*, 30, Summer 2008.

Viktor E. Frankl, *Man's Search For Meaning: The classic tribute to hope from the Holocaust*. London: Rider, 2004.

Daniel Gorenflo & James McConnell, "The Most Frequently Cited Journal Articles and Authors in Introductory Psychology Textbooks," in *Teaching of Psychology* (1991) 18: 8–12.

Barry Gribb, The Rough Guide to The Brain (Rough Guides Reference Titles). London: Penguin, 2007.

Sheila Hale, *The Man Who Lost His Language: A Case Of Aphasia*. London: Penguin, 2007.

Julia Heiman, Joseph LoPiccolo & David Palladini, *Becoming Orgasmic: A Sexual and Personal Growth Programme for Women*. London: Piaktus, 2009.

Headway, Factsheets from http://www.headway.org.uk/Factsheets.aspx accessed 8/8/2012

—— *"Coma stimulation: suggested activities."*

—— *"Completing the DLA claim form."*

—— *"Hormonal imbalances after brain injury."*

—— "Post-traumatic amnesia (PTA)."

Elisabeth Kübler-Ross, *On Grief and Grieving: Finding the Meaning of Grief Through the Five Stages of Loss*. London: Simon & Schuster, 2005.

Guilherme Neves, Sam F Cooke. & Trim V Bliss, "Synaptic plasticity, memory and the hippocampus: A neural network approach to causality" in *Nature Reviews Neuroscience*, (2008) 9 (1): 65–75.

Jean Piaget, *The Language and Thought of the Child* (3rd Ed.). Translated by Gabain, R. & Gabain, M. London: Routeledge & Kegan Paul, 1959.

Jean Piaget, *Comments on Vygotsky's Critical Remarks Concerning The Language and Thought of the Child, and Judgement and Reasoning in the Child*. Translated by Parsons, A. (Hanfmann, E. & Vakar, G. Eds.). Massachusetts: The MIT Press, 1962.

Psychology World, *Stages of Sleep*. Retrieved 8th August 2012, from http://web.mst.edu/~psyworld/general/sleepstages/sleepstages.pdf.

Trevor Powell & Kit Malia, *The Brain Injury Workbook: Exercises for Cognitive Rehabilitation*. London: Speechmark, 1999.

Trevor Powell, *Head Injury—a practical guide*. London, Speechmark, 2004.

Vilayanur S. Ramachandran, *Phantoms in the Brain: Probing the Mysteries of the Human Mind*. London: Harper Perennial, 1999.

Vilayanur S. Ramachandran, *The Tell-Tale Brain: Unlocking the Mystery of Human Nature*. London: Heinemann, 2011.

Giacomo *Rizzolatti* & Maddalena *Fabbri Destro*, "Mirror neurons" in *Nature Clinical Practice Neurology* (2009) 5, 24-34.

Oliver Sacks, *The Man Who Mistook His Wife For A Hat*. London: Picador, 1986.

Solihull Mental Health NHS Trust, *Mental Health Strategy*. Sollihull, 2005.

Endel Tulving & Fergus I. M. Craik, *The Oxford Handbook of Memory*. Oxford: University Press, 2000.

Andy Tyerman, *The Psychological Effects Of A Brain Injury*. Nottingham: Headway-the Brain Injury Association, 2006.

Lev Vygotsky, *Mind In Society*. John-Steiner, V., Souberman, E., Cole, M. & Scribner, S. (Eds.) London: Harvard University Press, 1978.

Lev Vygotsky, *Thought and Language*. Translated by Kozulin, A. London: The MIT Press, 1986.

Deborah Wearing, *Forever Today: A Memoir of Love and Amnesia*. London: Corgi, 2005.

Help

The Samaritans:

www.samaritans.org

08457 90 90 90

Headway:

www.headway.org.uk

0808 800 2244

Silverlining:

http://www.thesilverlining.org.uk/

0203 174 2051

Volunteer link up:

http://www.do-it.org.uk

Printed in Great Britain
by Amazon.co.uk, Ltd.,
Marston Gate.